MW00399100

Learn Hypnosis... *Now!*

Third Edition

By Michael Stevenson MNLP, MTT, MHt
Certified Master Trainer of Hypnotherapy

Learn Hypnosis… *Now!*
Third Edition

Dedicated to the love of my life, Kayla

Copyright © 2016 Michael Stevenson and Transform Destiny
ISBN: 0-9963334-2-8
ISBN-13: 978-0-9963334-2-9

Published by Transform Destiny
www.TransformDestiny.com

Table of Contents

Introduction

Welcome! You are about to embark on a fantastic journey. You will learn many things about hypnosis and the human mind along the way. It's a story of who we are and what we're capable of as humans, and how we can tap into it to better our own lives and the lives of others.

In this book, we will cover the theory and mechanics of hypnosis, five different styles of hypnotic induction, the structure of suggestion, hypnosis for therapeutic purposes (i.e., pain management, smoking cessation, weight loss, etc.), hypnosis for entertainment (stage hypnosis) and even self-hypnosis. We will also cover common myths about hypnosis. There are more than you know, and many that you probably believe to be true!

Hypnosis is a journey into the subconscious mind. It can be used in a variety of situations from having fun on stage or at a party, to relieving pain, to breaking habits, and even to achieving hypnotic anesthesia for surgery.

Prepare yourself for the ride of a lifetime – you're about to have some fun!

Who is This Book For?

This book is for anyone who wants to learn how to have more control over their life! If you have a desire to have fun, explore the human mind, understand the subconscious mind, learn how to give suggestions that work, and become more at peace with yourself, you have come to the right place.

Hypnosis is more than what we see in stage shows. It's more than 'hocus-pocus'. It's more than just showing off for friends and family. It's a journey inward. I offer you the opportunity to learn about the inner workings of yourself, as well as those of others.

Now, don't get me wrong... hypnosis is <u>fun</u> too! Children, teens, adults and the elderly each have their own style and charm in hypnosis. Stage shows, if done right, are humorous and fun for everybody. And you'll learn all about them in this book, too!

Can You Perform Hypnosis?

The simple answer is yes. Hypnosis is not regulated in most of the United States and the world*. Usually, no license is required to practice hypnosis. Hypnotherapy (the clinical use of hypnosis) is a self-regulated industry and, though there is no licensing, there are boards, such as the International Board of Coaches and Practitioners, which certify people in clinical hypnotherapy and more. If you plan to work with subjects as a professional hypnotherapist, see Appendix IV for information on

---

* Always check the law in your state or country. Laws change periodically. Your local chapter of the International Board of Coaches and Practitioners can assist you in interpreting the law in your jurisdiction.

obtaining certification for a career in Clinical Hypnotherapy.

There are certain rules and laws that govern acts used in hypnosis. For instance, certain issues should not be addressed without approval from the subject's physician or therapist. These issues will be addressed in the section titled "Should I Work With Everything?" in Chapter 3.

The most difficult part of hypnosis, initially, is finding subjects to practice with. I suggest that you keep your study of hypnosis quiet around people you know, at first. Those who know you best will likely be the most skeptical. Begin by asking a friend or family member to experiment in a, "relaxation technique," that you've learned and practice these techniques with them. Before they know it, they will be in a deep state of relaxation and hypnosis and will really enjoy the way it feels.

The first few times you practice hypnosis with others, you'll probably want to forget about giving suggestions to them, which you will learn about in Chapter 1. Just take them into a hypnotic trance state, let them experience the beauty and benefit of it, and then bring them out.

You will experience this for yourself, later in Chapter 1, when I explain how to download your sample hypnosis induction audio from our website.

Eventually, you can begin to let your friends and family know that you've been dabbling in hypnosis. At this point, you will have hypnotized a few people and become more confident in your own abilities. Confidence is a valuable trait to have as a hypnotist.

Conventions Used in This Book

Depending upon your specific context, you may be working with a client, patient, volunteer, audience member, relative, friend or guinea pig. Since I can't predict how you'll use your new skills, I'll settle on the word "subject," throughout this book when referring to the target of your hypnotic inductions.

New Words will be *italicized* to indicate that the word may be looked up in the Glossary (i.e., Now would be a good time to try some *convincers*.)

Within quoted text, *italicized* words are called embedded commands and are to be spoken with a different inflection, tempo or tone. This concept will be covered before the first occurrence.

Within quoted dialog or instructions, commands to you as the hypnotist will be enclosed with [square brackets].

About the Author

I am a certified Master Hypnotherapist, Master Practitioner of Neuro-Linguistic Programming (NLP, a related field), a Master Practitioner of TIME Techniques, a Master Success, Life and Business Coach, a Master Trainer of Hypnotherapy and a Master Trainer of NLP. I'm also the owner of Transform Destiny – one of the largest hypnotherapy, NLP and coaching training companies in in the world and Influence to Profit, a training company where we show business owners, marketers and sales people how to use hypnotic influence principles to succeed in business. I've been helping people change their lives and achieve their dreams since 1998.

I was not always a hypnotherapist. I used to be a computer programmer. I was a heavy smoker and had tried "everything under the sun" to quit smoking, with no results. After nearly fourteen years of smoking (the last four of those years trying everything to quit with no results), I quit smoking easily and effortlessly with a self-hypnosis tape that I bought at a stage show at the county fair.

I instantly became fascinated with hypnosis, but my first trip to the library yielded no results whatsoever. I began going from bookstore to bookstore looking for any information I could find on this incredible subject. Eventually, after I had read nearly every book I could find on hypnosis and NLP, I attended a live training, became certified as a Clinical Hypnotherapist and started my own private practice out of my living room.

I loved that weekend certification training so much, I purchased the rights to it and my company still teaches the course to this day.

Since then, my life has changed in so many incredible, amazing ways. My wife Kayla and I own and operate Transform Destiny (www.TransformDestiny.com), an NLP and hypnosis training institute, and Influence to Profit (www.InfluenceToProfit.com) a business training, coaching and mentoring company.

I have received hundreds of hours of hypnotherapy and Neuro-Linguistic Programming training and I am board certified by several prestigious boards.

I tell you this, not to impress you, but to impress upon you the fact that <u>anyone</u> can learn hypnosis. Even a former skeptical "computer geek" like me.

Since 2000, I've taught hundreds of thousands of people around the world hypnosis, NLP, TIME Techniques and coaching, either through my books, or in person.

These are, by far, my favorite subjects to discuss, and if you have a question, feel free to contact us any time at cs@transformdestiny.com, and/or sign up for our monthly newsletter at www.transformdestiny.com.

A Note About NLP: Neuro-Linguistic Programming

Throughout this book, I will reference the field of *NLP* or *Neuro-Linguistic Programming*. NLP is a related field which has been said by many to be the most advanced form of hypnosis available and is often called, "hypnosis with the eyes open."

NLP is a study of the mind, but it is different than the field of Psychology. While Psychology has mostly studied disorder, NLP finds examples of excellence and success and studies how the mind, the body, and communication (with self and with others) produce those results. If you could imagine having a "User Manual for the Mind," you'd be pretty close to the concept of NLP.

While the founders of NLP originally started by studying the world's greatest therapists to see how they produced rapid change with their clients, NLP goes beyond clinical training. It's a set of tools, techniques and beliefs that can help to propel you toward success in any area of life.

While creating the field of NLP, the co-founders studied Milton H. Erickson, probably the greatest hypnotherapist who ever lived. Erickson was able to hypnotize people in everyday conversation, without their awareness and greatly enriched both fields.

If you ever attend an NLP Practitioner Training, you will learn Ericksonian hypnosis, so you can hypnotize anybody just by having a conversation with them, as well as many other techniques for working with the human mind.

Part I
Fundamentals

Chapter 1: What is Hypnosis

In this chapter, we will take a look at what hypnosis actually is. While we don't _fully_ understand hypnosis from a medical/scientific standpoint yet, many studies are in process at the time of this writing that will shed light on exactly what this wonderful state is and how we can continue to use it in the future. Even though we don't know what it is, we do know that it works.

Here's what we _do_ know about hypnosis…

Hypnosis is a Natural State

The state of hypnosis – often called "trance" – is a natural state that each of us has the ability to enter. Some people are more talented than others at entering deep trance (this deep level of hypnosis is commonly called _somnambulism_). Everyone is able to enter this somnambulistic level of trance, but some enter it more easily than others.

Nearly every school of thought about mental health defines two major parts to the entity we call, "the mind." Some call it Id and Ego; some call it Child and Parent. The ancient Hawaiians called it Uhane and Unihipili. We will call them your Conscious Mind and Subconscious Mind (or Unconscious Mind, as many in this industry prefer to say).

Your conscious mind is the part of you that you're conscious of, the part of you that you "think" with. It consists of all of your conscious thought, and is generally limited to thinking of around seven things at any one time, give or take one two (7±2 "chunks" of information).

Your conscious mind makes up a documented 0.006% of your mind, while the subconscious mind makes up the other 99.994%.

Your subconscious handles the many millions of details that you encounter every day of your life. Your subconscious is the domain of your emotions. It's where your learnings and memories are kept, and it maintains all your perceptions, learnings and habits.

A good analogy that I like to use is that of a sailing ship. The Captain is your conscious mind, and does all the logical, rational thinking. It makes conscious, informed decisions based on the external and internal information in the moment. It does not deal with the lower-level, more mundane tasks. That's the Crew's your job. If you haven't guessed it yet, the Crew is your subconscious mind.

If the captain wants the ship to turn right, he doesn't grab the wheel and do the work himself! He gives the command, "All Hands! Full to Starboard!!!"

Something as simple as turning the boat right seems like an uncomplicated process. But behind the scenes, crew members are scurrying to make the command a reality. There is a man who rings the chime to indicate a turn, which prompts engineering to fire up one of the motors, which requires more steam, prompting crew members to shovel and burn more coal, which needs still other crew members to replenish the coal. These men work hard and deserve a good meal, so there are cooks that make food that waiters need to serve. Others have to replenish the food supplies, sweep the floors, check the weather, monitor sonar and radar, plot courses and a million other tasks, all just so the Captain can give his next order.

The same is true in your mind. Something as simple as picking up a glass of water involves hundreds of muscle pairs. To consciously think of each group of muscles to flex and tense in just the right proportion to pick up a cup, neither dropping it, nor crushing it, is as delicate an operation as ballet. It takes the intent and orders of the conscious mind, plus the multi-tasking skill of the subconscious mind to pull it off.

Now, in order for any captain to be a good captain, he must pay attention to the feedback from his crew. Can you guess what happens when the Captain starts ignoring, or even worse, mistreating the crew? That's right… mutiny! And that's exactly what happens when some of us get out of *rapport* with our own subconscious.

There is good news, though! Just the act of using hypnosis begins regaining rapport between the conscious and subconscious minds. Hypnosis opens the channels of communication between the two, and when the subconscious gets its fair share of attention, it begins to produce better results.

Basically, hypnosis allows us to open the subconscious mind to suggestion, while the conscious mind wanders or is otherwise distracted.

Hypnosis is <u>not</u> mind control, brainwashing, black magic or voodoo. The hypnotist has no special powers over the subject. Hypnosis is actually a <u>cooperative</u> activity, which requires the full consent of the subject.

As a matter of fact, <u>all</u> hypnosis is <u>self</u>-hypnosis. The subject enters their <u>own</u> trance, the hypnotist merely guides the subject through his experience and offers suggestions to the subconscious mind along the way.

You Have Already Been Hypnotized

You may not know it, but you've already been hypnotized!

Have you ever been daydreaming, so oblivious to the world that you didn't even hear someone speaking to you or calling your name? Have you ever read a book or watched a movie and got so into it that you lost all track of time and feel as though you are there, live in the story? Have you ever been driving down the road and suddenly, "snap to," wondering how you have traveled the last few miles?

These are all altered-states, called, "book trance," "movie trance," and "highway trance." During this time, your subconscious mind has taken over while your conscious mind wanders.

In essence, you have been hypnotized! You just didn't know how to use that state for a purpose!

The Signs of Hypnosis

People react to hypnosis in many different ways. Because of this, no simple table can accurately describe every reaction to hypnosis. Some people appear to be, "out cold," while others will have fluttering eyelids or some other types of twitching. Young children, who are actually in altered states most of the time, will squirm or even giggle while in hypnosis.

The point is that hypnosis is completely subjective and just because one person may or may not show one or more of these signs does not necessarily mean that the subject is or isn't hypnotized. The following three levels of trance are simplified and not really meant to signify concrete states of hypnosis. More will be said about this in the section titled "The Stages of Hypnosis".

Figure 1.1 - Signs of Hypnosis

Light Trance	• Deep relaxation • Change in respiration • Fluttering of the eyelids
Medium Trance	• Face Flaccid • Redness and increased lacrimation of the eyes due to relaxation of the muscles around/in the eye • Labored breathing
Deep Trance	• *Catalepsy* • Inability or unwillingness to speak

The Effects of Hypnosis

Measuring the effects of hypnosis is another topic which is highly-subjective. While there are some similarities in the experiences of most subjects, none of these effects are either a requirement or a direct indication of successful hypnosis. People will feel their own subjective feelings in hypnosis, so this is only a guideline.

Figure 1.2 shows some of the common effects of the hypnotic state.

Figure 1.2 - Effects of Hypnosis

Deep Relaxation	Most subjects will experience an intense feeling of relaxation. Although, relaxation is not necessary for trance, many methods of hypnosis promote trance through dissociation with the body. This is usually done through deep relaxation.
Floating or Sinking	Many subjects report the gentle feeling of floating or sinking into the chair or couch that they are on.
Increased Senses	While hypnosis usually involves dissociation from the body, typically, many people report that they also become aware of certain things through an increase in the sensitivity of their senses.
Amnesia	Many people experience amnesia about the content of the hypnotic experience. This is actually encouraged, and even intentionally suggested, when using hypnosis in a therapeutic setting.
Time Distortion	Trance can do some amazing things to a person's perception of time. Many sessions that last an hour feel like ten or fifteen minutes to an awakened subject. Sometimes, twenty-minute sessions feel like hours. Time distortion is completely subjective. Everyone experiences it differently.

The Stages of Hypnosis

Hypnosis is generally regarded as having three levels or stages of "depth." There is a fairly heated argument between different camps regarding the actual levels (even if there actually are any levels) of hypnosis and what characteristics belong to each level. This chart is based on the work of Leslie LeCron and the LeCron Depth Scale, which is still in use by many hypnotists today.

Figure 1.3 - Stages of Hypnosis

Light Trance	• Feelings of lethargy and relaxation • Catalepsy of the eyes • Catalepsy of the arms or other muscle groups • Floating or sinking feelings • Full body catalepsy
Medium Trance	• Smell and taste can be suggested. For example, making an onion taste and smell like an apple • The ability to totally erase or block numbers from the mind • *Amnesia* of certain events • *Glove Anesthesia* • *Analgesic* suggestions • Post-hypnotic suggestion
Deep Trance	• Automatic movement • Positive hallucinations can be suggested. For instance, in my hand, you will see a tennis ball. What color is it? • Complete anesthesia • Negative hallucinations, while more difficult to suggest than positive hallucinations, can sometimes be suggested at this point. For instance, the chair you are sitting on has just disappeared... you can no longer see the chair anywhere • Comatose, or what has been commonly called, the Esdaile state

Bear in mind that these stages are very fluid. Please, do <u>not</u> get the idea that only a person in medium trance can receive post-hypnotic suggestions, or that only a person in deep trance can experience anesthesia. Everyone is different and people respond in different ways to hypnosis. This table is only presented as a loose outline and is <u>not</u> meant to limit your options in any way. Remember, Anything is possible!

Dispelling Myths About Hypnosis: Common Questions

Let's face it, Hypnosis has not fared well under the skeptical eye of most. There are many reasons for this, media being the biggest, in my opinion.

The image of hypnosis most commonly put forth by Hollywood is one of magic, mystery and power. In these movies, some sinister villain usually waves something shiny in the "victim's" face and gains full and complete control.

This is all entirely false. The reality is that you will always be in complete and total control in hypnotic trance. While the trance state does allow one to have more influence over the subconscious mind than the awake state, there are built-in protection mechanisms that will prevent a person from succumbing to negative suggestions from others. So, in order to help people to trust us and relax sufficiently, we must dispel a few myths about hypnosis before we begin working with them.

Most uncertainties about hypnosis stem from subjects' beliefs that they will lose control and be made to bark like a dog or something of the sort. I will provide some specific ways to combat these fears later in this book, but for now, let's look at some of the most common questions people have about hypnosis and the ways that I like to answer them.

Will I Fall Asleep?

No, you will not fall asleep. While many people may look "zonked out" while in trance, this is usually just a product of the extreme relaxation and comfort felt during hypnosis. Remember, hypnosis is not sleep. At all times, you will be completely awake and in control, but you may be so relaxed that you don't choose to move because it's just so darn comfortable.

Will I Lose Control or be a Zombie?

Not at all. Hypnosis is a cooperative activity, which means that you must <u>consent</u> to all suggestions in order to accept them. If I were to suggest something that would make you uncomfortable, cause harm or is out of line with your morals, you would either come out of trance, or simply ignore the suggestion. You are <u>suggestible</u> under hypnosis, but not <u>commandable</u>! Your subconscious mind will always protect you, and will always choose to adhere to your morals.

If That's So, Why do People in "Hypnosis Stage Shows" Bark Like Dogs and Act Like Fools?

Have you ever known anyone personally that has gone on stage? The stage hypnotist plays with a bit of a stacked deck. Think about it. Who goes up on stage? Volunteers do! These are people who <u>enjoy</u> hamming it up! Heck, I'll bet if you watch most of them volunteering, they were probably standing on their tippie-toes on their chairs saying "Me, me, me, me, me, me, pick meeee!!!!" They enjoy the attention! Chances are they might bark like a dog even if they weren't hypnotized just to get a laugh!

This is not meant to take <u>anything</u> away from stage-hypnotists. Stage hypnotism is an extraordinary art that is difficult to master. And, in order to put ten to fifty subjects under trance in less than five minutes, and then have them do entertaining things, it definitely helps to have the right type of subjects.

What Will Hypnosis Feel Like?

Hypnosis can feel radically different to different people, so I can't tell you exactly what you'll feel. But I can tell you this, it will be completely comfortable. You will relax completely. And, you will have a profoundly incredible and positive experience. The best way to learn about it is to <u>experience</u> it.

What if I Can't Be Hypnotized?

Everyone <u>can</u> be hypnotized. This does not necessarily mean that everyone <u>will</u> participate in hypnosis. Remember, hypnosis is cooperative. The subject is <u>always</u> in charge. But rest assured that anyone with an I.Q. above that of a cucumber, who can relax, comprehend and follow simple instructions, can be hypnotized. The only way it wouldn't work is if you resisted it. So play along and have fun!

What If I Get "Stuck" in Hypnosis?

This is the most common fear of the average person. It's also the silliest. In the entire history of hypnosis, no one has ever gotten "stuck" in trance. You've never become permanently "stuck" daydreaming, have you?! Of course not! While a few people are reluctant to "snap to," just because hypnosis is so relaxing and feels so good, everyone comes out of hypnosis feeling great, refreshed and full of life.

<u>*Time for Your First Trip*</u>

As I said before, the best way to learn what hypnosis feels like is to experience it. Now that we've taken all the mystery and hocus-pocus out of hypnosis and dispelled all the common myths that you used to believe, you get your chance to <u>do just that</u>.

As my gift to you, I have made a special hypnosis recording so you can feel exactly what this wonderful thing called hypnosis like. There are no silly suggestions in it (such as suggestions to buy more products or take my live trainings) just a few suggestions for peace of mind and relaxation. So find a nice place to sit down and enjoy it.

Simply log on to the website using the link on the next page and download the MP3 audio file, which is free to you as an owner of this book. Please be mindful that the audio file you are about to download is copyrighted material and should not be shared with others who have not purchased this book. Listening to the recording constitutes your acceptance of the terms in Appendix VI.

While hypnosis itself is not dangerous, closing your eyes and trancing out while driving, or doing some other activity that requires your attention, obviously is dangerous. So the standard warnings apply: do not use while driving any type of vehicle, operating machinery or power tools, babysitting or parenting or performing any other activity that requires your attention.

This is a simple induction using relaxation techniques and guided imagery. There are a few suggestions for general happiness and well-being, then you will be brought back out of trance. Allow yourself about 30 minutes of quiet, peace time where you can be alone and undisturbed. Follow the link below to begin.

www.LearnHypnosisNow.com/free-hypnosis-session

Induction Types

Overview

The field of hypnosis is as varied as any of the other "helping" professions. There are many different styles of hypnosis in use today. It probably won't surprise you to know that the style most commonly portrayed by Hollywood, the media and mystery writers is the style that is least likely used by real, knowledgeable, professional hypnotists.

Let's take a look at five common styles of hypnotic induction: Permissive, Authoritarian, Dave Elman style, Milton H. Erickson style and Rapid Induction. Although some may argue it until they are blue in the face, my belief is that none of these are mutually-exclusive. Each style has its own advantages in different situations. As a matter of fact, most inductions are a mix of styles. So don't artificially limit yourself by learning only one style.

Authoritarian

Authoritarian style is the style that you most often see from Hollywood or read in horror/mystery novels. Using this style, the hypnotist literally commands the subject into hypnosis.

> "Close your eyes. Take three deep breaths and begin, now, to relax every muscle in your body. Go deep asleep!"

This previous passage is indicative of an authoritarian type of induction, and commands like this would continue to be given until the client went into trance, many times out of sheer boredom. This sort of style usually works on people that like to be told explicitly what to do. Stubborn people, skeptics, defiant people, those with polar-reactions and people with otherwise "strong" personalities are probably not good candidates for an overly authoritarian induction. Many people simply don't like to be told what to do or respond poorly to authority.

Permissive

Permissive techniques are much less commanding. Instead, you speak in a much more indirect way that makes the subject feel like they are making the decision about what he or she wants to do.

There is virtually no emphasis on the "power" that the hypnotist has over the subject (because, if you remember, the hypnotist has no power over the subject!) Use of *embedded commands* is common to clue the subconscious mind into what it is you want them to do. Embedded commands are commands that are "hidden" within normal conversation. The command words themselves are said with a slightly different tonality or tempo to mark them out to the subconscious mind.

"If you would, sit down in a comfortable position. I wonder if you can begin to *relax completely*. It feels good to relax, doesn't it? You might be able to notice that your eyes are getting heavier and your eyelids will soon feel very, very tired. Please *close your eyes* and listen to my voice."

In the above example (embedded commands were italicized for emphasis), you can see that the mood is much more permissive and polite than the Authoritarian approach. At all steps, the subject is asked or suggested to do things, not told. This technique can appear to be similar to the Erickson style of hypnosis, on the surface. This is the type of hypnosis taught in this book.

Ericksonian

Milton Erickson was a man who truly understood how to communicate with the subconscious minds of others. Nearly everything he did communicated on multiple levels. In order to communicate that effectively, you need to learn to use everything around you in your communication, from the subject's history to events and noises around you at the moment, to the responses your subject has to your commands. That is why this style of hypnosis is often called *utilitarian*.

For example, if someone inadvertently came in through the door during a session, many new hypnotists would panic and think the session was a failure. Milton would have simply said something like:

"…And as the doors to *your subconscious* open… they allow you to *go even deeper inside…*"

Much like a phony fortuneteller, one of the keys to this style of hypnosis is deliberate vagueness. Ericksonian techniques use vague statements and fuzzy descriptions to *pace* the subject's ongoing reality. In other words, to match what the subject feels at the moment to create more of a reality.

For example, Erickson might look at you and say:

"Sometime, maybe very soon, you will blink…"

When you eventually do (as, of course, will happen) he will say:

"That's right… And that will allow you to relax even deeper…"

Or he might say:

"In a moment, you'll begin to feel a sensation in one of your hands… Maybe one will be lighter or heavier than the other… Maybe you'll notice that one is warmer or cooler than the other…"

This will cause the subject to become curious and withdraw to ponder the situation and check his hands. Of course, no two hands are alike, so the subject is **sure** to feel <u>some</u> difference, and he will believe that this is the one Milton speaks of, causing him to go even deeper into trance!

This serves two purposes. First, it serves to pace the reality of the subject, thereby creating a greater level of rapport, trust and belief. Second, and most important, it begins to get the subject into an altered state by occupying the subject's conscious thoughts and causing him to withdraw.

Learning Ericksonian hypnosis is advanced and highly recommended once you get the basics down. These "conversational hypnosis" patterns aren't only for use in a clinical setting. They can also be used in everyday communication with anybody, from speaking to your kids to closing a sale.

Elman

Dave Elman discovered a rapid approach that works very well on most people. While hypnotists at the time were worried about *eye fixation* and achieving "natural" eye-closure before inducing hypnosis (sometimes taking an hour or more), Dave Elman simply asked for it. His theory was that hypnosis is a state that we're all capable of and familiar with, so induction could be rapid. Elman dispensed with all the pretense that was so rampant in hypnosis at the time, and developed a way of hypnotizing people very deeply in just a few minutes.

Elman's technique was so powerful that he taught it almost exclusively to doctors, dentists and psychotherapists. There are detailed records of him curing stuttering, migraines, sinus problems and asthma, over and over. He could also gain perfect anesthesia for performing surgery using hypnosis is just a matter of moments. This technique is so powerful, the famed Mayo brothers performed more than 17,000 deep abdominal surgeries using Elman's method with no use of chemical anesthesia, at all.

The Elman method is one of the most advanced forms of hypnosis and hypnotherapy. Because of that, it's out of the scope of this introductory book about hypnosis. It is so advanced, that we don't even teach it in our basic NLP Practitioner Certification trainings, but rather our NLP Master Practitioner Certification training. You will receive plenty of content in this book to get started with basic hypnosis, and if you love it as much as I did, you may want to continue your education in live courses to get the advanced trainings.

Rapid Inductions

Rapid inductions can be very powerful when used in the right situations. The key to performing successful rapid inductions is to use them at times when other factors contribute to the success of the induction. Here are a few examples:

Highly Hypnotizable Individuals: Sometimes, very suggestible subjects can be hypnotized using rapid induction techniques. These are the types that are so suggestible that they often trance out just watching someone else go into trance!

Shock: Very useful in the medical fields, is the shock induction. Consider a situation where a patient comes in to the E/R in shock, such as a compound fracture, and you simply don't have time to administer anesthetic, and maybe you can't calm the patient sufficiently to work on the affected area. Simply jumping toward the patient with arms and hands out and screaming "SLEEEP!" is often enough to put the subject in a mild trance, because of the already altered state of shock they are in. This approach is obviously extreme and not recommended for most subjects. It could, as a matter of fact, get you punched, or cause your patient to have a heart attack. Use at your own risk!

Social Proof: *Social Proof* is a very powerful concept that has been studied for years by social psychologists. Have you ever noticed that people tend to do what they see other people doing? Ask a question in a crowded room that requires a show of hands. For the first four or five seconds, you'll get no response – nothing. Then maybe one or two will raise their hand. Seeing this, more raise their hands, and so on. Most didn't feel comfortable answering until social proof dictated that it was acceptable to do so.

Social proof is used a great deal in stage hypnosis. There are usually a variety of people on stage at any given show. By the time they've been on the stage two minutes, the experienced stage hypnotist already knows who the joker is, who the reserved one is, who will be their star, who is willing to try on clothes of the opposite sex or stuff balloons under their shirt, etc. But most importantly, he knows who is the most suggestible. By concentrating on getting these easiest people into trance first, he is setting up social proof that works with him as he moves down the line to the more difficult subjects. In most shows, after the first four or five people are tranced out, all the hypnotist has to do is look at a subject, yank their arm, and say

"Sleep!" The anticipation and social proof is enough to put them in trance.

Veterans of Trance: Trance is a skill. We can all do it to some extent, but some people are naturals or very experienced at it. For most of us, the more we get to experience trance, the better we get at it and the faster and deeper we can go. People who have experienced trance and know what it feels like can easily put themselves back into that state with little or no help from the hypnotist. Rapid induction works well for these people, especially if you've previously given them a post-hypnotic command to go back into trance upon command.

Children: Children are notorious for their imaginations. Imaginary friends, imaginary worlds (my kids come up with imaginary promises that I supposedly made!) They walk around much of the time in an altered state, because of this, it's usually very easy to get a child into trance using a rapid induction. Most children simply won't respond to longer, more boring inductions anyway, and rapid inductions can be made fun to kids at any age.

Interventions

I'm going to says something now that may shock you: Nobody is ever cured with hypnosis. That's right. Hypnosis is not in itself a **cure** for anything.

Instead it is a tool, and a very powerful one at that, that allows you to speak directly to the subconscious mind of your subject. It's not the hypnosis that gets results, it's the suggestions that are given in hypnosis that get results.

The part of the process where suggestions are given is called the *intervention*. Without the intervention, hypnosis is essentially just meditation (yes, they are both the same state.)

It's what you say at this point that will dictate the intention and the result of the session.

The Value of Pre-Written Scripts

There are many varying opinions about hypnosis scripts. Some hypnotists think that scripts are useless because they're too generic and don't target the specific needs of the subject. Some believe that scripts are fabulous because they are tried and tested, over and over, otherwise people would not be distributing or selling them.

I tend to take the middle ground on this issue. I believe that scripts are a great starting point. Many times, especially for beginner hypnotists, scripts are the only way to get a start. After all, in the beginning, you usually need some inspiration!

Please notice that I said scripts are a good starting point. I believe that scripts should only be used to get a general idea of what to do, and should not be read word for word, otherwise you may "mis-match" your client.

For instance, if your subject already has their eyes closed, it can be counter-productive to be continually telling a subject, "your eyelids are getting heavy… soon, you will notice your eyes closing…. Your eyelids are slowly closing." Yet, this type of mistake is possible if you're reading verbatim from a script and not paying attention to your subject. This could be very annoying to the subject, causing them to come out of trance.

The most important thing you can do is to be "in tune" with our subject. Pay attention to their physiology and body language and tailor your session to match. This will get you the best level of rapport and help your subject go into the deepest trance possible.

Visualization and Future Pacing

Visualization and Future Pacing are two concepts which are similar and related. Both are ways that you can reinforce suggestions made during the intervention to your subject.

Often, a perfectly good suggestion can crumble under real world conditions. For instance, someone who has had suggestions for smoking *cessation* may do wonderfully as a non-smoker until Friday night when they go out drinking with friends at the club, and the pressure of the real world becomes too much to handle.

This is where visualizing becomes important, if not essential. The idea is to have the person visualize, as vividly as possible, a time in the future where they have the success they desire. They will visualize themselves with all the new resources they've acquired (i.e., the ability to refuse a cigarette or eat sensibly or possess self-confidence), and to experience themself using those resources successfully. Any form of visual imagination is considered visualizing.

Future Pacing is a specific kind of visualization. The difference is, rather than painting our own image of the future, we interview the client to find out details about how they envision themselves enjoying their success in the future. Then, under hypnosis, we help them create the scene, hear the sounds and feel the feelings of success as they described it.

This allows the subject to mentally experience their success immediately. The key is to have them realize success in the safely and comfort of your presence instead of in the real world, which is full of pitfalls and temptations.

There's another benefit to doing this, because you can immediately get valuable feedback from your client. If they had trouble imagining the success, you may want to rehypnotize them and give them key suggestions again. It's better to spend the time in the first session than to have the subject struggle and come back later.

Other forms of visualization can be very useful as well. Visualizations can help to calm and relax the subject and there are even studies that show that visualization can activate powerful healing mechanisms in the body.

Suggestions

Suggestions are the heart of a good hypnotherapy session. Without suggestions, this would just be meditation. Good, clear and concise communication is key to giving successful suggestions, which the subject will accept.

Here are some pointers to get you started.

Be congruent: When giving someone a suggestion, the pitch and tone of your voice should always match your intended meaning. For statements, your tone and pitch should remain relatively flat or constant. For commands, your pitch should go down slightly at the end of your sentence. For a question, your pitch should go up at the end of your question. This may seem like common sense, but you wouldn't believe how many beginner hypnotists forget tonality and say something that reads like, "In a moment you'll be a non-smoker?" Not only does it confuse the subject but it also makes your suggestion less effective.

Be Thorough: Make sure that you specify exactly what you want. You are speaking directly to the subconscious mind, which can interpret things very differently than the conscious mind.

If you are working with someone who wants to lose weight, your initial reaction might be to suggest, "From now on you will eat less."

This suggestion may seem perfectly acceptable to you. But, remember, you're hearing this with your <u>conscious</u> mind. To the subconscious mind, this could mean something as silly as taking one less bite per meal. Or worse, the subconscious could interpret this as "From now on, I'll only eat once a month." As you can see, being thorough is important.

In our previous example, a better suggestion might be "From this point forward you will only have the urge to regularly eat healthy foods. Chocolates, candy and fatty foods will only be eaten moderately or on special occasions. You'll decide when your meal is done based upon need and fullness only. After taking each bite you will consciously check your stomach to see if you need to eat more. You'll stop eating when you are pleasantly comfortable, at six on a scale of one to ten, with one being hungry and ten being full." As you can see this suggestion leaves very little to interpretation and will net much better results than a vague suggestion.

Be Positive: I cannot stress this enough. Because of the way the human mind works, we cannot process negative statements subconsciously.

For instance, I could say, "Don't think of chocolate chip cookies!" What did you just think of? Chocolate chip cookies, of course! You can't think about what you don't want to think about without thinking about it. Think about that!

Our minds are very symbolic. We think in symbols of pictures, movies, sounds and feelings and have to turn words into these internal "experiences" to understand them. So, when we interpret a negative communication, the brain first makes an Internal Representation (a picture, sound or feeling) of the thing that is being discussed in order to even understand what is being said.

For example, have you ever noticed that when someone tells their child, "Don't spill that milk," within a matter of moments the child will knock over the glass? The parent's simple error was that they didn't form a positive suggestion to their child. The child made a movie of spilling milk in their mind and the body acted on it. In effect, they <u>gave</u> their child a hypnotic suggestion, and the child accepted it! You could say, it's the <u>parent's</u> fault the milk was spilled.

A more productive suggestion might sound like the following, "Be sure to keep your glass upright," or, "Please keep your milk either in the cup or in your mouth," or even simply, "Be careful with your milk."

Speaking positively may sound funny, at first, because we are so symbolic. We tend to make a picture or movie of what we don't want to happen in our mind, and then turn it into language which includes the words not or don't. It's just the way our minds work when we speak. But it's not a very efficient way to communicate with others.

So, as funny as positive language may sound at first, it's <u>much</u> more powerful and influential to do so. You may have to get a little creative to come up with good wording, but the fact is, positive suggestions are easier for the subject to understand and have a far greater chance of being accepted for what they are.

The simple trick is to imagine what you want, instead of what you don't want. Then, the language becomes much easier.

<u>Stack Suggestions:</u> *Stacking suggestions*, is the act of stringing suggestions together so that the subject has less of a chance of rejecting the group of suggestions.

In general, people want to please. We usually like to please people and will respond to simple requests because it feels good. But if you ask request after request after request, your subject may tell you to take a hike for asking for so much of them.

The key here is to "stack" suggestions. If you stack your suggestions correctly, you stand a much better chance of influencing the other person.

Suppose you ask your child to pick up their bike. When they're done, you ask them to close the garage. You've asked the child to do two, individual things, which they will evaluate separately and they may or may not reject one or both. Maybe they'll pick up their bike and forget to close the garage, or close the garage and forget the bike. Maybe they'll forget both.

Now, consider this phrasing: "Please close the garage when you pick up your bike." You've now stacked these two suggestions. Your child will have to evaluate these suggestions as a whole, and because of our amenable nature, will most likely accept it.

Assumptive Language: One quality that can you're your suggestions more powerful is *Assumptive Language.*

For example, if I'm speaking to a potential client, I might say, "You will really enjoy the feelings you experience when you go into trance". I'm assuming a few things here. Of course, I'm telling the subject will have feelings that will be enjoyable. But in order for that to happen, we must assume (or presuppose) that the client will willingly and successfully be hypnotized by me, because the assumption in the sentence is: "<u>when</u> you go into trance" (not if).

This is a trick that is used quite often in sales when an employee will walk up to you and say "Would you like to pay for that with cash or charge?" They didn't ask you if you want to <u>buy</u> it, they're presupposing that by asking you a question that <u>assumes</u> you will buy it. In essence they are saying, "I know you are going to buy that, so how would you like to pay for it?"

When using hypnosis, strive to be as assumptive as possible. The conscious mind has a very hard time rejecting these kinds of statements.

Stack Realities: Another example of stacking or layering is to *Stack Reality*. This is frequently called "pacing reality" and has been used in sales under the name of *Yes Sets*. This is a bit of a combination of the last two techniques.

When stacking realities, you state things that are apparently obvious and verifiable to the subject, things where the subject can <u>only</u> say yes, to persuade them to say yes to the suggestion you <u>want</u> them to accept. It is difficult for a person to discount one part of a sentence if they have agreed to the other parts.

For example I could say, "You're sitting there, reading this book, learning about hypnosis, thinking those thoughts, feeling those feelings, and as you continue to breathe like that, and you suddenly want to <u>get every training available from Transform Destiny</u>."

What I've cleverly done is called stacking realities. There are six verifiable statements of reality in the previous sentence, and one suggestion which I <u>want</u> you to accept. By stacking realities, I've gotten you to say, "Yes I'm sitting, yes I'm reading, yes I'm learning about hypnosis, yes I'm thinking thoughts, yes I'm feeling feelings, yes I'm breathing" and out of sheer repetitiveness and habit, you will probably also agree that, "Yes, I want to get every training available from Transform Destiny!"   ;)

Metaphor

Stories have been used since ancient times to teach, entertain and heal. In the field of hypnotherapy, a metaphor is a type of story that has specific, personal and therapeutic meaning to the subject. Metaphors are usually short stories that, when interpreted at the subconscious level, give new resources or solutions to the subject.

In one famous example, Milton Erickson was working with a man who wanted to lose weight and who's favorite hobby was gardening. So he struck up a conversation with the man about his garden. Milton eventually stated that the tomato was his favorite plant, because when you planted the seed, the tomato took just the right amount of nutrients and fluids – no more and no less – and grew to it's perfect, natural size.

Now to the conscious mind, this is a friendly conversation, or a story about a garden. But to the subconscious mind, which takes everything personally, this story wasn't about gardening at all. The subconscious mind stepped into the role of the tomato and accepted the suggestions to eat and drink just enough to become a desirable size. The man subsequently lost weight.

The structure and creation of therapeutic metaphors is more advanced than we can cover in this small, introductory book. Until you learn NLP, you can buy script books that have metaphors for various topics.

Neuro-Linguistic Programming (NLP)

Neuro-Linguistic Programming is a field using very powerful techniques that is closely related to hypnosis and hypnotherapy. It has often been described as, "hypnosis with the eyes open." It produces results that are incredibly fast and long-lasting.

It's got a funky name, so let's look at what that means:

Neuro: Having to do with the neurology, or the nervous system, and how we experience our world though our senses: visual (vision), auditory (hearing), kinesthetic (touch), olfactory (smell) and gustatory (taste).

Linguistic: Having to do with our language, both internal and external and how it affects the makeup of our thoughts, held as pictures or movies, sounds, feelings, smells, and tastes plus our self-talk.

Programming: Programs, patterns and systems that we run within our mind.

So, Neuro-Linguistic Programming is how we use the language of the mind to program ourselves and assist others in creating an extraordinary life. NLP is used to model excellence, eliminate negative emotions, destroy limiting beliefs, undo limiting decisions and create a compelling future.

If you've ever watched the movie *The Secret* you probably walked away feeling really inspired, but having no idea what to do. For example, the movie tells you to "ask, believe and receive," to have anything you want in life.

But <u>how</u> do you believe? Belief is a deep subconscious function that most people don't have the tools to change.

In terms of personal development, NLP gives you the mechanics to change your beliefs, your thoughts, your behaviors and so much more.

In terms of business, NLP gives you the tools to <u>take any venture</u> to the next level and beyond, by being able to communicate more thoroughly with prospects, clients, staff, partners and vendors.

In terms of therapy, NLP trainings can certify you as a Practitioner or Master Practitioner of Neuro-Linguistic Programming to work with others professionally as a coach and/or therapist.

Coupling hypnosis and NLP can be very beneficial, sometimes making the difference between a subject's success and failure. Oftentimes, NLP can be used in lieu of a hypnosis intervention, as in the rapid-change techniques used for curing phobias, using hypnosis only to future-pace the subject and reinforce the treatment.

NLP is considered an "extension" of hypnotherapy, because it has taken many of the best parts of hypnosis and improved it to the point where "trance" is literally unnecessary.

I always look at it like this: The more "tools" you have in your toolbelt, the better you will be. The more techniques that you can use at your disposal to help your clients, the more likely they are to have a massive shift in their life, resulting in happier clients, better results and more cash in your pocket.

NLP is not just a field but can be a way of life. It has created radical success in my life, and the lives of many of hundreds of thousands of people I have coached and trained.

To learn more about NLP for free, visit www.FreeNLPHomeStudy.com where you can watch my 10-hour Intro to NLP course, complimentary.

Summary

There are many different styles and techniques at your disposal. Each has its own strengths. None of them is just hypnosis alone, but they all make up hypnosis together. In the next chapter, we'll begin to look at some of those techniques in depth.

Part II
Techniques

Chapter 2: Pathways into Hypnosis

Overview

You've made it this far, so congratulations! You are *this close* to learning how to actually hypnotize people!

In this chapter, we actually get into the meat of hypnosis. You'll learn the words of hypnosis and how to say them, the attitude that you should have, as well as what to do when people are in hypnosis. This is where it really starts to get good!

Tonality

One of the most common questions asked is, "What voice should I use to hypnotize people?"

Contrary to popular belief, and the bologna you might read in some other books, the pitch of your voice (the "highness" or "lowness") is not very important to induce trance! Otherwise, most women (and many men!) would be inherently bad hypnotists.

The two most important vocal qualities to be concerned with are *tonality* and *tempo*. Tonality deals with the qualities of your voice, such as smoothness, volume and even emotional overtones rather than the pitch, while tempo describes the speed and rhythm of your words.

It's important that you convey feelings of relaxation and carefree-ness in your voice by using a soft, half-whisper half-speaking voice at a low- to medium-volume and a slow, methodical tempo.

Think of how you might read a bedtime story to a small child. In my hypnosis trainings, I always play an audio clip of the old Taco Bell® commercial where the Chihuahua dog, in a hypnotic voice says, "Your getting verrrry sleepy… No wait, you're getting verrrry hungry…"

Just be sure to convey with your voice the state you want them to enter. A study done years ago shows that the words you say are only about 7% of your total communication. The tone of voice and body language are much more important at 93%. So if you quickly yell at them in your most irritating, nasal voice, "YOU'RE GETTING VERY SLEEPY!!!" they will surely do just the opposite. So, slow it down, and use a nice, quiet, soft voice.

Congruence

The effects of the *congruence* of the hypnotist are of utmost importance. Because hypnosis is a cooperative venture, the hypnotist must *believe* wholeheartedly that the subject will go into trance and accept suggestions. If there is any major doubt in the hypnotists mind, it will be communicated to the subject non-verbally. Therefore, if the hypnotist doesn't believe that something can be fixed or accomplished using hypnosis, your chances are for success become much more difficult.

This concept extends directly to you. Be sure that your body language, vocal tone and attitude all reflect the probability and certainty of the suggestion you're giving the subject, otherwise the subject will pick up on your incongruence. I'm not saying that you have to <u>believe</u> in the suggestions, just that you convey the attitude that your subject can carry out the suggestion. For instance, I can do past-life regressions, even though I don't necessarily believe in past lives. The important thing is that I believe past life regression can help the subject if <u>they</u> believe it will help them. Just keep an open mind, and, as my grandmother used to say, "Fake it 'til you make it."

Performing Suggestibility Tests

There are a few standard "tests" that many hypnotists perform. Traditionally, it has been taught that these tests prove how suggestible a person is. I tend to think they serve a much greater purpose.

In my opinion, the real reason to perform these "tests" is to prove to your subject that they can be hypnotized – not to prove it to you. Success breeds success, and so when your subjects accomplish these seemingly amazing, yet incredibly simple and automatic, feats, they will be that much more confident in your skills as a hypnotist, and in their skills as a subject.

While the results of these tests are nearly automatic to all but the most resistant of subjects, some people simply will not perform. Just as success breeds success, failure breeds failure, so remember three important points when performing these tests:

Don't call them tests! It is amazing how a person's perspective on an activity changes as soon as you label it a "test"! Simply calling anything a test can cause people to panic, to have anxiety or to become concerned and distracted with the results. Keep these exercises simple and low-pressure by calling them "experiments" or "games" that will allow them to experience a little bit of hypnosis. I like to call them "Fun Experiments for your Subconscious Mind."

Don't divulge the details of the test. Simply begin the tests without going into detail about what outcome is expected. This will keep the subject from declaring the test a "failure" if they don't think they've met the expected outcome. It will also keep them from faking the results, and then later saying it didn't work because they were just trying to make you happy. If they don't know what the result is supposed to be, you can frame the outcome in any way you want.

***Everybody* Passes.** These are not tests, so there's no reason to grade anyone. Let success breed more success, even if it's just the illusion of success. No matter how they performed, even if not at all, tell them that they did a great job and that they're **excellent** hypnotic subjects. Since you've kept the details of the tests secret, they have no reason to doubt your judgment.

Make it fun and make it about *them*. Rather than making this about how much supposed power you have over them, make it all about them. Tell them this will show them how much power they have over <u>themselves</u>. Also, do this with a little bit of flair and make it fun. The more fun you make it, and the less of a power challenge you make it, the more they will be willing to play along and let things work.

<u>Suggestibility Tests</u>

These are some of the scripts used for suggestibility tests during a typical session. Text in italics is referred to as an embedded command. These will be covered in detail later, but for now, just remember that they are meant to be said with a slightly different tonality or tempo, so as to mark out the command to the subconscious mind.

Introduction

So, I've explained to you the basics of hypnosis, what you'll experience, what you'll feel, so let's just do a couple of neat little experiments with suggestibility and you'll be able to see what it's all about. You'll be able to see exactly how much power your imagination has over your body.

The Lemon Test Script

"Let's begin by just sitting in your chair, very relaxed, with your eyes closed, feet on the floor, and hands in your lap... Very good."

[Note to Hypnotist: Make sure that they follow your instructions. If at all possible, provide an example by yourself sitting down, feet flat, hands in lap and relax. The best way to provide a suggestion is to lead by example while instructing.]

> "Imagine yourself, now, sitting in your most comfortable spot in your living room. You can *feel the comfort of home* as you lounge in your favorite chair or couch... Wherever you may be... Seeing those familiar things... Hearing those sounds... And feeling those feelings of... *home*."

[Note to Hypnotist: Pause for a moment to let these images and feelings sink in. There is a dual purpose to this introduction. First and foremost, we want to kick start the subject's imagination. We are showing them the power of their imagination, so we want to create as vivid of a picture/sound/feeling as we can, while using very general terms so that we don't mismatch our subject's memory of their actual home.

The second reason is that, as we describe this scene, the subject will "go inside" and begin to experience the sights, sounds and feelings of home. This will increase your rapport automatically by causing him/her to be as comfortable as if they were in their own living room.]

> "Just imagine what it's like as you begin to put your feet to the floor and stand up. Feel the texture around your feet and toes... Feel the muscles in your legs supporting you... Feel the weight of your clothes upon you as you begin to walk toward the kitchen."

[Note to Hypnotist: This is simply more imagery to guide the subject into an internally oriented state. Pause briefly (three to five seconds) to let them absorb the details and catch up.]

"As you enter the kitchen and begin to make your way toward the refrigerator, you can feel the cold hardness of the floor beneath your feet… take in the sights of the room… And smell the smells that your kitchen has. You gaze at the door to the refrigerator as your hand reaches out to grasp the cold, hard handle."

[Note to Hypnotist: Just continue to flood their senses with sight (visual), sound (auditory) and feeling (kinesthetic).]

"You tug on the handle… Resisting at first… then you hear that familiar peeling sound as the seal around the door pulls away, the door comes open and the inner light floods out. You peer inside to find a bowl of perfectly ripe, vibrantly yellow lemons. You can hear the refrigerator fan turn on as you feel the cold air breezing out past your face.

"Reach out and take a lemon from the bowl. And as you *feel the cold bumpy rind of the lemon, firm in your hand,* close the door and begin making your way to the counter, where you'll see a rather large knife and a cutting board.

"Place the lemon on the cutting board and pick up the knife. Feel the weight of this knife in your hands. Hold the lemon and begin to cut down the middle. Feel the juice spurting out on to your hands as you see the lemon split in half. Smell that lemony smell… Mmmmm. Pick up one half of that lemon. See the light glinting off of the inside, cut that half in half again, leaving one quarter of a lemon. You can hear the flesh of the lemon tearing as the knife slices through. Pick up that quarter lemon… feeling some juice running down your hand as you pick it up… see the light glistening off the flesh of the lemon… bring it up to your lips and take a **big, juicy bite**!"

[Note to Hypnotist: Pause here for a second. Watch the subject's mouth pucker, as it invariably does, and say…]

"Open your eyes. Do you notice an increase of saliva in your mouth?"

[Note to Hypnotist: Nod your head "Yes" while asking this question and look the subject right in the eyes. This will help the subject realize that they should be thinking, "Yes". The truth is that most people are not aware of how much saliva is in their mouth at any given time, so if you ask this question convincingly, they will most likely answer (and believe) "Yes"… even if they don't have more saliva in their mouth. This will amaze them and show them the power of their own mind over their body.]

"You have just experienced the power that your mind has over your body. You've taken a bite out of an imaginary lemon, but your body has reacted as though you have taken a bite out of a real lemon by puckering your lips and causing you to salivate!

"Was there really a lemon? Of course not, but your body thought there was! Hypnosis works so well, because it creates thoughts so realistic, the body reacts biochemically.

"Let's do a few more fun experiments!"

Finger Vice Script

"Let's go ahead and stand up, and begin by clasping your hands out in front of you, fingers laced, thumbs overlapping. Good. Now, point your two index fingers straight out towards me. Great, squeeze those fingers together as tightly as you can, because in a moment, they're going to return right to that same spot."

[Note to Hypnotist: Pause for about two or three seconds while they squeeze their index fingers together.]

"Now, open those fingers up as far as they will go, but keep the rest of your fingers clasped. I'm going to put a little hypnotic vice on your fingers… without touching you, I'll turn the little vice handles and clamp your fingers down, just like they were a second ago."

[Note to Hypnotist: With your hands at either side of their outstretched index fingers, begin turning imaginary vice screws like you would bicycle pedals, as if you were tightening a vice or a C-clamp around their fingers. They will watch with amazement as their fingers close automatically, without you ever touching them. This trick, while a test of suggestion, is helped a little by human physiology. The fingers are more comfortable at a resting position and will easily retract to that position with little need for help. Just the tiniest bit of suggestion starts them to clamping down.]

> "Just a few twists of the hypnotic vice and… Watch that spot just between your fingers get smaller and smaller as the fingers get closer… and closer… and closer!
>
> "There we go! Fingers clamped down. Excellent! Let's try another!"

Sway Test Script

> "Please stand straight up, feet together, and arms at your sides. Go ahead and look straight up to the ceiling, nose pointing straight up, and close your eyes. Great!"

[Note to Hypnotist: At this point, walk around to stand behind the subject and BRACE yourself, one foot in front of the other, as if you were going to push something heavy or catch something heavy.

For this test, you'll want to place your hands near the subject's shoulders at all times to prevent them from falling (which would break all that good rapport you've just built!) Remember, some clients are funny about being touched, be sure to stay away from the chest area with your hands and always let the subject know before you touch them if their eyes are closed.]

> "Imagine that you are on a small boat, sailing in the sea. You can smell the salt in the water and see the beautiful blue sky. It's a windy day and you can feel the waves rolling under the boat up and down, back and forth, back and forth. You feel yourself swaying back and forth, backward and forward as the waves get bigger… and bigger… back and forth, back and forth and…"

[Note to Hypnotist: with your hands on their shoulders, pull gently with your fingers so they fall backwards <u>toward</u> you, *ever so slightly*. Just an inch or two is plenty.]

> "Very good!"

[Note to Hypnotist: This test is another that is helped a bit by human physiology. The average person cannot stand with their feet together, hands at their sides and nose pointed straight up without swaying at least a little bit. So time your "backs" and "forths" to the subject's movements, if in fact they are moving.

When you reach the point where you pull their shoulders, be sure to do so *ever so slightly*, especially with their eyes closed. **Be sure to do this while they are swaying backward and not forward**, otherwise their movements will be working against you! Don't fight the laws of physics, because physics will win. If the subject is already swaying backward toward you, you shouldn't have to pull hard at all, just a little tap should do. The subject should very easily and very lightly fall backward just an inch or so before you catch them with your hands on the back of the shoulders. Then gently push them back straight up to help them get their balance.

It is extremely important to remember to brace yourself. I've seen tiny, tiny women subjects bowl big brawny men over because the men were standing with their feet side-by-side instead of front-to-back and had no stable base to stand on. No matter how big or small your subject is, always stand ready.]

Heavy/Light Arms Script

"Excellent! Let's do this one. Sit back straight in your seat and hold your arms straight out in front of you like a zombie. And just go ahead and shake out the arms. They don't have to be totally relaxed, but you can keep them out there relaxed. Good... Close your eyes... And now I want you to pick one hand… it doesn't matter to me... Whichever one wants to, and just turn it over."

[Note to Hypnotist: It is important that you remember to have the subject *close their eyes first*, then turn over the hand. We are going to show them that their hands/arms will move through sheer suggestion. By having their eyes closed, they won't even realize that their arms have **already moved apart**, just by turning one over. This way, if the subject does not respond for the rest of the test, you still have some results to show. Just act like they did a great job and congratulate them. Remember, success breeds success.

For the purpose of our discussion, we are going to assume that our subject has turned over their right hand.]

> "Excellent! Now, I want you to imagine that I have a large book in my hands. This is the biggest, heaviest old book from the back of the library. It's got big, thick, yellowed pages, and a heavy leather cover. You can smell the dust on the old, thick pages. And you can hear that thud as I put that book in your right hand now."

[Note to Hypnotist: don't touch their hand or arm, this will make them think you pushed their arm down rather than hypnosis]

> "You can just *feel the weight of that book now*... pushing your right arm down, as it gets heavier, and heavier. That book just gets heavier and heavier and the arm keeps going down, down… down.

> "Good. Now, *imagine* that I am tying the biggest, lightest bunch of helium balloons you've ever seen to your left wrist. Notice the weight of the arm completely disappears as the balloon goes up and up, gets lighter and lighter. As the string pulls taught, the balloon catches the wind and begins to pull the arm up, higher and higher. It's getting lighter and lighter.

"*Yes... Feel the weight on your right arm* as I place another big, hardbound dictionary on that hand - the kind that you might find in a big library - *feel the weight* as I stack that on top of the other book with a big thud... that's right... *Pushing that arm down...*

"And at the same time, you can *feel your left arm begin to float up* higher and higher as I add a few more super-light helium balloons to the bunch and they *float up, up, up into the sky*. Your left arm becomes lighter, and lighter as the balloons take over and *raise your arm.*"

[Note to Hypnotist: Keep repeating these types of suggestions - adding books, adding balloons - until you have a pretty good distance between the top and bottom hands. Four or five inches is sufficient. If you have continued for more than one and a half minutes and seen no results just continue with the next paragraph and show them the inch or two that the hands parted when they turned over their hand in the beginning.]

"Now... Open your eyes... Look at your hands!"

[Note to Hypnotist: Wave your hand between their hands, if there is enough room.]

"Notice the amount of space between your arms! Isn't that amazing?! See? The human mind can create change in the body just by imagining!"

You should have a pretty good idea of how suggestible your subject is by now. This will help you gauge your persistence and style during your induction and interventions.

Eye Fixation

Just a quick note about eye-fixation. You may read books that tell you that eye fixation is the most important thing to hypnosis. In my opinion this is a very outdated belief.

While eye fixation was considered very important in earlier forms of hypnosis, it has been found that it only serves to tire the eyes and to focus the subject some. It does not <u>induce</u> hypnosis. While eye fixation can be a useful tool, it is not necessary, as some classic books insist.

In the old days, hypnotists would work for as much as an hour to get eye closure through fixation. Often times using a pendulum held above the eye line that the subject would look up at, and would continue, even if their subject had entered trance in the first five minutes. I prefer to skip all of the pretense and just ask... "Please close your eyes, now."

Some scripts may incorporate eye fixation, and that's fine – there's nothing inherently wrong with trying to get natural eye closure by fixating the eyes, but don't let it take over the session at the expense of everything else.

Inducing Trance with Hypnotic Inductions

Overview

Now for the part you've probably been itching to read. This is where we learn how to actually put people in trance! There are several common styles of induction, but we will focus on the easiest and most common in this book, Progressive Relaxation. No single style is better than any other. Rather, each style has its own benefits in different situations with different subjects.

Knowing which style to use with which subject will, of course, come with training, time and experience. As you quickly become comfortable with this script, you'll probably want to learn other styles.

The Elman and Erickson styles of hypnosis rarely involve scripts. In fact, they work best without scripts, so it helps to learn how to speak hypnotically without a script.

The following script can be used word-for-word, as long as you are paying attention to the subject. This means, for instance, if their eyes are already closed, you would skip the part about closing the eyes. Embedded commands will be italicized and my comments/instructions to you will be shown in brackets.

You're Getting Sleepy – The Progressive Relaxation Script

"Just *relax*... And sit back... And *close your eyes*... Good... In a few minutes, you're going to be more relaxed than you have <u>ever</u> been before. I'm going to start mentioning certain parts of your body, and as I do, I want you to feel that part of your body *just begin to relax.* That's right... just *feel* that part of *your body begin to relax.*

"Start by imagining yourself... laying on a hammock, or perhaps a bed, or maybe a pile of leaves in a wonderfully peaceful, safe... beautiful forest. The sky is a spectacular hue of dark blue as dusk begins to turn to twilight. There are no sounds of the world... except the gentle breeze... the lazy song of a few crickets... And the hypnotic bubbling of a nearby brook.

"Now... Imagine a glow beginning to form at the top of your head... This is the most relaxing and peaceful light you have ever seen... and as that light begins to slowly move down the body, it *completely relax*es every muscle, nerve and fiber that it gently touches."

[Note to Hypnotist: Now we begin by progressively relaxing the entire body. Notice that we use terms such as "the arms" or "the back" as opposed to "your arms" or "your back". This is done to help facilitate the dissociation so important to hypnosis.]

"This wonderfully relaxing glow begins, now, to grow... And engulf the top of the head. You can feel the entire scalp *let go* as it begins to *relaaaaxx...* Even the hair seems to be relaxing. This beautiful light grows even more... And as it begins to touch the forehead, you can feel all the little frown lines disappear as each muscle lets go... Good. It begins to engulf the area around the back of the head... ears... All the little muscles around the ears *relax...* cheeks... nose... And the eyes... *relax...* and each and every little muscle around the eyelids *relaaaxes* completely. So much so that *you don't even want to open them...* that's right.

"Going down deeper now, the glow begins to grow down... to the lips... *Relaxing...* And your mouth... and your jaw *relaxes...* So much so, that the teeth might even part a little... Very good... And this fabulous glow of comfort... And relaxation... just engulfs the entire head.

"Moving down, you can feel the relaxation down the back of the neck... Into the shoulders and the middle of your back as the shoulders begin to droop comfortably... This peaceful feeling begins to grow... Down the spine... Radiating out through the back from every vertebrae... Like little antennas, broadcasting relaxation throughout the back... And moving into the lower back now... Completely *relaaaaxxed...* completely comfortable.... Mmmm...

"This incredible feeling… Makes it's way around the hips as the light grows down into the legs… the hamstrings becoming *soooo relaaaaxxed*… working it's way down past the backs of the knees… Into the calves… Around the bottoms of the heels… And even the bottom of the feet are now *completely relaxed*… As this relaxing glow embraces the muscles. There are no worries… No cares… Only a few moments of total peace… total relaxation.

"Excellent… Doing so well now… Begin, now, to see that glow growing down from the chin… and relaxing down the front of the throat… down the neck… Relaxing every muscle… Every nerve… and every fiber… As it continues to spread through to the fronts of the shoulders… Down into the upper arms… And past the elbows… the forearms… the wrists… hands… and each and every finger… just completely *relaxed*… As you *go deeper*… Good.

"Now the light continues to *go down*… Growing into the chest… Relaxing all the muscles of the chest… Even the lungs begin to relax with every breath of this glow… In…out…in…out…in……"

[Note to Hypnotist: Time the previous with their breathing. Then pause and just pace their breathing with your own for about 10 seconds. On the final breath, say with a sigh…]

"Relaxing… It *feels so good* to relax… And to know that no matter how deep you go, you can always *go deeper*…

"Going further down now... Passing the solar plexus and saturating the midsection... All the muscles in that area *just relax...* Very good... and the light continues to grow... Into the hips, so relaxed. Into the upper legs... the quadriceps like a mass of loose... limp... rubber bands. So comfortable... Still growing... Over the knees... shins... ankles... the tops of your feet and each and every toe completely comfortable... completely relaxed... No worries... No cares... today is in the past and tomorrow is a million miles away."

[Note to Hypnotist: Pause here for about eight to ten seconds to let your subject soak in and contemplate quietly.]

"As you begin to float to your feet, and take in the wonderful sights of your forest, you notice a beautiful stone stairway leading down into a safe, serene valley of total peace and relaxation. This staircase will lead you into a profound state of deep, deep hypnosis. We're going to go down these stairs now, and as I count backward from ten to zero, each number I say will take you even deeper, and deeper, and even deeper."

[Note to Hypnotist: Pause for about five seconds, then begin counting, with each number very spaced out.]

"Ten... taking that first step now... Nine... Eight... Going deeper... Seven... And deeper... Six... Five... No worries...

No cares... Four... your are going into a deep state of
hypnosis now... Three... Almost to the bottom... Two...
tired to even move. One... total peace... total relaxation...
Aaaaaanddd....Zerooooooo....."

[Note to Hypnotist: By this point, your subject should be
pretty well in trance. How deep will be different for each
client. From this point, you might do convincers,
suggestions, and then bring them out of trance. We'll learn
more about these techniques soon.]

Now that you know what to say, go find some friends or
family who want to experiment with a "fun relaxation
technique" you learned and practice!

Hypnotic Aids

There are many aids (and gimmicks) out there that claim to
help you achieve trance. Some are useful, some not so
useful. I'll cover a few here and give you my take. This is
just my personal opinion, so make your own decisions and
feel free to choose whatever works for you and for your
subjects.

Using Music to Aid Your Induction

Music is one of my favorite trance tools. Nothing calms
the nerves and puts people at ease quite like music. There
are all different kinds of music that can be used.
Everything from Classic to New Age can be used, but I
wouldn't recommend anything strong like rock, punk or

heavy metal. The idea here is to soothe the subject, not pump them up!

I recommend Hypnotic Trancescapes. I created Hypnotic Trancescapes, which incorporates deep hypnotic and psychological techniques that assist you in achieving trance for yourself or for your subject. The music you heard earlier in the sample induction is Hypnotic Trancescapes. I designed the music to complement a complete hypnotic session from beginning to end, so it's one hour of continuous music that has a track for hypnotic induction, two tracks for the middle, and a final track to come back out of trance.

You can read more about Hypnotic Trancescapes at www.trancescapes.com.

Pre-Recorded Inductions

There are some hypnotists who prefer to leave their subjects with a pre-recorded hypnotic induction. The clients listen to it through headphones, and then the hypnotist returns at the end to give the actual suggestion.

As far as I can tell, the only benefit is to the hypnotist (who must just be way too busy to deal with his pesky clients!). The subject loses out on a number of levels. First, the induction is not customized to the subject. Just the same as reading a script verbatim, a pre-recorded induction doesn't cater to the non-verbal signals given off by the subject.

My suggestion is that you stick <u>with</u> your subject through the entire session, pay attention to their verbal and nonverbal signals, and deliver an induction suited to their individual needs.

Mechanical Hypnosis Aids

While some devices have been scientifically tested to facilitate Alpha patterns in the brain, I believe they are mostly expensive gimmicks. With flashing lights or white noise, these devices are supposed to automatically produce trance in the wearer. While there may be some validity to that claim, I still think it's best to be with your client and give them the personal experience of a customized hypnotic induction.

<u>Rapid Induction Techniques</u>

Post-Hypnotic Suggested Induction

This technique is for subjects whom you have already hypnotized. Post-Hypnotic Suggested inductions are a convenient way to get returning subjects into trance.

The idea is to associate a word, a look, or a touch with the trance state they are in on their first visit so that you can easily put them back into that trance state, without having to do a slow, boring relaxation procedure again.

Here's an example to use when your subject is already in trance:

"It feels sooo good to relax like this... And I'm going to show you the quickest way for you to get back to this <u>wonderful</u> state. Upon awakening, and for the rest of your life, any time you hear me say the word platypus and touch you on the knee... <u>any</u> time I say the word platypus and touch you on the knee… you will immediately sit down, close your eyes and go deeply into hypnosis. Again, the moment I say the word platypus and touch you on the knee, you will sit down, close your eyes, and go deeply and immediately into trance..."

Next time you see them, this combination of word and touch will have them relax, collapse and go deep into trance in just seconds. This is very useful for follow-up sessions.

Pattern Interrupt – The Handshake Induction

Have you ever been walking along a sidewalk and taken a step off of a curb that you didn't know was there? Or unexpectedly tripped over something you didn't see? That hazy, confused state that you experience for the following few seconds is the result of a *pattern interrupt.*

A pattern interrupt occurs when a thought process that has been completely internalized into an subconscious action gets interrupted. Walking, for instance, has most likely become a program that is run completely by your subconscious mind. Of course, you make a conscious decision to walk somewhere, or in a specific direction, but you don't actually think to yourself, "Tense this muscle to move my leg forward, then straighten my toes, put foot down, lean forward. Now, tense muscles in other leg..."

Having to consciously control all the muscles for walking in this way would take an incredible amount of conscious thought, so the brain packages complex operations, such as these, into subconscious programs.

When one of these "programs" gets interrupted, the conscious mind becomes confused while the subconscious is left grasping at straws for what to do next. This produces a very short, light trance, and it's a very convenient time to offer a quick suggestion or two to the subconscious mind.

That's the theory behind one of Milton Erickson's most famous inductions.

To begin, Milton would simply hold his hand out, inviting a handshake. In America – especially in business – we shake hands all the time. We've done it so much that shaking hands has become a subconscious process. Think about it, Most of the time, you don't even look at the other person's hand. Your hands just reach out and automatically meet in the middle.

As the subject's hand moved forward, Erickson would very casually and subtly, so as not to be perceptible, lower his hand a little. This leaves the subject grabbing at air, and interrupts his "pattern."

In the following seconds, Erickson would begin to slowly push the subject's outstretched hand towards their face and say, "Look at your hand... And notice the changing focus of your eyes... the color and texture of your skin... As you *close your eyes... Relax...* And *go deep inside...*"

The suggestions start very small, so as not to alert the subject. "Look at your hand," is a very small suggestion. But by stacking a few small suggestions in succession, Milton would get the subject into a nice, light trance.

Shock Induction

Shock inductions <u>should not</u> be used as an everyday induction. Frequently, in emergency situations, such as an accident scene or a hospital E/R, victims can become hysterical and jeopardize their own care by not communicating with doctors or not sitting still during an examination. Patients presenting with compound fractures are frequently brought into the E/R in this condition.

The shock example is simple. The idea is to overload the subject's sensory system. Simply jump out toward the subject with hands and arms outstretched and yell, "SLEEP!!!" This is often sufficient enough to put them into a light trance.

This induction should be used only in emergency situations that you have been trained to handle. There are various issues that can cause this to be dangerous. If your subject had heart a condition or other health issues, a shock induction could be very dangerous. Use your best judgment and, as with everything in this book, use at your own risk.

Awakening Your Subjects

Awakening your subject is often a great mystery and the source of many people's fears. Contrary to popular belief, awakening the subject is one of the simplest tasks in performing hypnosis. Often, all that is required to awaken the subject is to "count them up," as in the following script:

> "In a moment, I'm going to count from one to five. As I do, and with each number I say, you will come twenty percent of the way back into the room, back to wakeful awareness."

[Note to Hypnotist: Increase volume and strengthen tonality with each number.]

> "One, Beginning to notice sounds in the room. Two, Noticing a sensation in your hand or your foot. Three, take a nice big deep breath. Four, take a nice big stretch. And, five, eyes open, wide aware, feeling wonderful and refreshed."

This is just one example. There are limitless ways to bring people out of trance. In my opinion, it is best to use a gradual approach, like this, instead of a hard and fast, "When I snap my fingers, you'll wake up" type of awakening. If you wake your subject up too quickly, they can become disoriented, just like if someone woke you up from sleep too quickly.

 As far as subjects getting "stuck" in trance, it is impossible. Nobody in the history of hypnosis has ever gotten stuck in trance. There are, however, infrequent cases where the subject is so relaxed, so comfortable, that they just don't heed your command to wake up. There are three possible solutions to this, and at least one of them has always worked:

- Gently shake the client's shoulder and say something like, "Mr. Smith, your time is up now. It's time to go out in the world and do good things."

- Gently shake the client's shoulder and say something like, "Ms. Smith, it's time to go now, or I will be forced to charge you another hour at double the rate."

- "Mr. Jones, if you do not come out of trance, I promise you I will never take you this deeply again. I will never let you experience the beauty of this wonderful feeling again."

Part III

They're Hypnotized... Now What?

Overview

There are many things you can do once you or your subject are in trance.

First, we will cover the therapeutic aspect of hypnosis, commonly called hypnotherapy. In this chapter, you'll learn how hypnosis is used to help others.

Next, in Chapter 4, we will cover self-hypnosis where you'll learn how you can improve <u>your own</u> life through the power of your subconscious mind.

Finally, in Chapter 5 we will cover stage hypnosis and how to use hypnosis for entertainment.

Chapter 3: Hypnotherapy

Warning: I cannot stress this enough. You should receive the proper training before working with other people for therapeutic purposes. Doing therapy without proper training can actually cause more problems than it can fix. This book serves as a jumping-off point into the world of hypnosis, and the completion of this book is in no way an endorsement of your ability to conduct therapy. Neither the author nor the publisher can be held responsible for information you learn from this or related material.

When you're excited enough to learn how to use hypnosis with others, I highly suggest you take a live training and become certified like I did. There are many training institutes that teach hypnotherapy including mine, Transform Destiny, where you can become certified in clinical hypnotherapy in a live course, or through home study. Visit www.LearnHypnosisLive.com for more information.

Deepening the Trance

Once you have gone through the hypnosis induction, your subject could be at any level of trance from superficial to deep.

There are several ways to deepen a trance. Many clever suggestions can be made up to take your subject deeper and deeper into the trance state.

The technique taught here, called *Fractionation*, is probably the most widely used technique and is very effective.

As you have already learned, trance is a skill. Some subjects are naturals, but it stands to reason that, if practiced, any subject can get "better" at trance. In the old days, hypnotists would go for session after session without doing any therapy at all! The first several sessions were merely "practice runs," where they would let the client get better and better at trance. Sometimes, it would take a client up to 30 sessions, spaced a week apart, before the therapist would consider them a "good" hypnotic subject capable of deep trance.

Then, it was discovered that there is no real need to wait a week between trance inductions. The client could be awakened, then re-hypnotized within minutes or seconds and receive the same deepening benefit as if they had waited a week. This process, called fractionation, allows the subject to achieve deeper and deeper levels of trance with each induction. Let's look at an example that can be used word-for-word once the subject is already in trance:

"Very good... Feeling sooo relaxed, now... In a moment, I'm going to count from 1 to 5. As I do, and with each number I count, you'll become more alert, more awake. Then, when I snap my fingers and say, "Sleep," you will relax, collapse and go deep asleep twice as deep as you are right now. Again, I'm going to count you up from one to five, you will awaken more with each number until you are awake with the number five. When I snap my fingers and say "Sleep," you will go down even deeper - twice as deep as you are now. One, two, three, four, five, *snap* sleep! All the way down now... that's right. Twice as deep."

This technique can be used many times in succession, as often as necessary, but I generally like to use it three to four times to get the subject into a deeper trance. The number of times you use it is up to you and will be based on your subject's current state and the desired level of trance.

Convincers

Convincers are one of the most important, yet overlooked, techniques in hypnosis and adding them can take a person from being an "average" hypnotist to a "great" hypnotists.

Convincers serve three important purposes and should be a part of every session you perform. The first purpose of a convincer is to indicate the level of trance to you, as the hypnotist – to convince you that the subject is in trance. If the client is not deep enough to carry out these simple suggestions, you'll probably want to use a deepener like, fractionation.

The second purpose of convincers is to actually convince the **client** that they are, in fact, hypnotized, in the moment. When they perform these hypnotic techniques, the results will convince them they are in trance, and actually deepen the trance, because of that conviction.

Finally, the third purpose of convincers is to convince the client that they were in trance, **after** the fact.

Since hypnosis is such a radically different experience from the idea most subjects have built up in their imagination, they will often doubt that they were "hypnotized" and will need some convincing.

They will often come out of trance and say things like "Well, I don't think I was hypnotized, because I could hear everything you said." This is why it's important that you always both **a)** explain hypnosis fully before doing any work with a client and **b)** Do your convincers - <u>every time</u>!

You'll give your subject suggestions that their eyelids are heavy, their arm is heavy, and their other arm is light. This will prove to both you and them that they are in trance.

This way, when the subject says, "I'm not sure I was hypnotized..." you can say "Well, your hand floated, didn't it? You weren't able to lift your arm, were you? See? You <u>were</u> hypnotized and you did excellent!"

Doing convincers is generally a quick process, as long as things go well. Each convincer <u>must</u> be passed before you continue. If you continue the session without successful convincers, your client will not be convinced (actually, they will be convinced that the hypnosis <u>didn't</u> work), and then they may ruin the results by their own negative suggestions to themselves. If your subject fails a convincer, deepen their trance and do the same convincer again, until they pass.

You will want to do the convincers right after you do the induction. Just flow into them. No introduction or explanation is needed. At this point, it's also a good idea to change the tone of your voice from the softer, hypnotic voice into a more conversational and slightly authoritarian voice.

While you can get creative and make up your own convincers, I like to stick with these classics. These convincers are called Heavy Eyelids, Heavy Arm, and then Light Arm.

Heavy Eyelids

"In a moment, I'm going to count from one to five... As I do, your eyelids will become a hundred times more relaxed than they are, even now... So much so, that they just won't even want to open... Try as you might and find out with a little bit of delight that they just won't open. That's right... One... feeling how completely relaxed your eyes can be. Two... Feeling the weight of your eyelids... Three... eyes becoming so heavy... Four, too relaxed to even open... And, Five... Eyelids feeling like they're glued together. Now, go ahead and try… try in vain to open your eyes only when you're sure that *you cannot.*"

[Note to Hypnotist: Pause briefly, but continue after you see about two or three seconds of movement. Usually, the eyebrows will bounce around a bit and the eyes will stay closed. If you see no movement at all, that means they are so relaxed that even the surrounding muscles didn't move. Wait about ten seconds and move on.]

"Good, that's enough... Just relax the eyes... The eyes are returning back to normal now, only ten times more relaxed. Good."

Heavy Arm

"In a moment I'm going to count from one to five. As I do, and with each number I count, you'll begin to notice your left arm is getting heavier and heavier... So heavy, that you won't even be able to lift it. You'll try and find out with a little bit of delight that it just won't move. One... absolute relaxation of the arm... as... Two... You begin to notice the weight of your arm on your leg... And... Three... Feel the weight of the arm pressing down on your lap... Heavier and heavier... Four, too relaxed to even move... And... Five. The arm is just so heavy. Now, try in vain to lift your arm as you notice that *it's just too heavy.*"

[Note to Hypnotist: Pause briefly, but continue the second you see attempted movement in the arm – usually around the shoulder - or after 10 seconds]

"That's enough... that's right... they're just too heavy. The arm is returning back to normal now, as you relax even deeper..."

Light Arm

"Now, as you *begin to notice your right hand* feels slightly different from your left, you'll be shocked to find out that *your right hand is beginning to feel quite a bit lighter.* That's right, your arm feels like it's full of helium and lighter than air as it begins to slowly, float off of your leg with honest, subconscious movement. You can notice it getting lighter and lighter as more helium gets pumped in with every… breath… you… take…"

[Note to Hypnotist: Time these last four words with the subject breathing in. The arm tends to naturally lift a bit as a breath is drawn and the chest expands, so this will help to solidify the suggestion.]

"Very good, as it continues now… Getting lighter and lighter…"

[Note to Hypnotist: Repeat these kinds of suggestions until the arm is three to six inches above the lap.]

"Excellent, and the arm can just stop… Floating comfortably, right where it is.

"Now, when *you're ready to make this change now*, allow the arm to just drop comfortably to your lap sending you ten times deeper than you are, even now.

[Note to Hypnotist: Wait for the arm to drop]

"That's right…"

Using Direct Commands

While *direct commands* seem to be a part of every induction in Hollywood movies, they are actually only part of the intervention in hypnosis. In many cases, using <u>only</u> direct commands such as "you will quit smoking" are simply not enough to overcome a smoking addiction by themselves. The client will usually need a fitting metaphor and some future pacing (both discussed later) to get deep, long-lasting results.

I am <u>not</u> saying that direct commands are useless. They are very effective when used in conjunction with these other modes of trance-therapy. Let's look at a few examples of direct commands.

- ***With*** each breath you take, your urge to smoke will become less and less until it is completely gone. Just let it go...

- From this point forward, you are a healthier person - eating foods that are good for the mind and good for the body - and you avoid and reject foods that tend to promote excessive weight gain.

- On the count of three, your fear of heights will be gone. Although you will retain a healthy common sense about safety at any height, you are comfortable in high places and be able function normally and in good spirits at those heights.

Many people ask me how to come up with direct suggestions. And the answer is, let your intuition do it. In our live trainings, students are always surprised at how easily this comes.

The most important thing is to remember that the subconscious mind does not process negatives. So you direct commands should always use positive, suggestive language. Tell them what you <u>want</u> them to do, not what you <u>don't</u> want.

In other words, instead of, "You don't want chocolate cake," which makes them think of eating and wanting chocolate cake, you would want to say, "You choose natural, healthy foods and enjoy eating them at each meal."

You can also ask your client, "Is there anything you'd like for me to suggest to you while you're in trance?" This question reinforces the fact that the client is in control by giving them a part to play in the suggestions given.

Metaphor

A therapeutic *metaphor* is a story that relates to your subject (and their problem) on a subconscious level. They're simply stories that your subject's subconscious mind can learn from.

For instance, a child who always cries crocodile tears when it doesn't its way may be told the story of "The Boy that Cried Wolf". A woman who feels that she is trapped in an abusive relationship might be told about an escape from a prison camp in World War II. A teen with a limiting belief may be told a story about a paralyzed boy who learned to walk again. A man with self-esteem issues may be told a story about how every culture is unique as a people, and there's nothing wrong with being "different."

The subconscious mind is naturally very good at drawing connections between self and the characters, actions and relationships in a metaphor, even if they don't consciously know the story is about them.

The therapeutic metaphor is usually a story that is not meant to be understood by the conscious mind. On the contrary, they are often designed to confuse, distract or otherwise misdirect the conscious while the subconscious mind draws parallels and derives meanings from the story in relation to its current dilemmas.

Entire books have been written on the subject of metaphor. Therapeutic metaphors are an excellent means for hypnosis inductions and interventions. While a true discussion of metaphor is beyond the scope of this book, the bibliography has excellent references to books that have metaphoric scripts, and books that will teach you how to create effective metaphors for your clients.

End-Result Imagery and Future Pacing

No matter how good your therapy is in person, your subject still has to go out and "perform" in the real world. Expecting a client to integrate all that they have learned in your presence well enough to be able to use those new resources immediately in the real world – which is filled with real pressures and challenges in real situations – is not always realistic. Your subject needs a "practice run" in the comfort and safety of your presence and the chance to install, integrate and test their newfound resources in an appropriate situation.

Future pacing is how you do this, and it's a simple process. You just paint a picture for the client of what they will see, hear and feel when they have success. Here's an example:

> "Now, picture yourself, in the future, in a situation where someone will offer you a cigarette. Notice how it is now that you turn it down. It feels so good inside, and you can hear the voices of the people around you as they praise you for becoming a non-smoker."

This allows the client to fill their future "timeline" with success. The subconscious mind is very much like a train on a track. If you lay the track toward success, it will just keep moving that direction.

This is a very powerful technique. But, as powerful as it is, there is at least one way to make it more powerful...

End-Result Imagery

End-Result Imagery is a specialized version of future pacing. Instead of making up a successful future situation for the subject, we will first interview the subject and ask them what they think they'll be doing when they're successful. This allows you to operate from within their, "model of the world," as we say in the field of NLP. You'll be using their own imagination of what the future will look, sound and feel like, making it all the more powerful.

How to Use End-Result Imagery

The reason we call this technique End-Result Imagery is because we want to construct vivid imagery of the "end result" of their therapeutic change, based on their "desired result of how their life will be affected once they have their new resources. Extracting these ends values from your subject's answers is easy. There are three questions to use when interviewing your client's for End Result Imagery.

1. **What will you be doing when you _____ (quit smoking, lose weight, sleep better, have better concentration, etc)?**

Your subjects will most likely give you a state or a feeling here, such as, "I'll be happy," or "I'll be healthy." You can take note of that state/feeling and even use it within their imagery, but what we're really looking for here are specific behaviors.

So, if they client says, "I'll be feeling healthier," you can fill in the blank and say, "Great, what will you be doing when you <u>feel healthier</u>?" Just ask the question again, but use their last response.

This can go 'round and 'round with some subjects. Don't get discouraged. Keep at it until they give you a specific behavior.

2. **Good, so if you're not _____, what will you be doing?**

Sometimes, your clients will give you behaviors that are based on a negative action. For instance, "What will you be doing when you lose weight?" - "Well, I won't be sitting on my butt." This may seem like a motivating answer, but for our purposes (imagery), it's difficult to picture yourself not doing something. So, in order to get a more specific answer, and to put it into a positive frame, we fill in the blank and say, "Good, so if you're **not** <u>sitting on your butt</u>, what will you be doing instead?" They may say something like, "Hmm... Well, I'd like to start kickboxing." This is a much better answer as far as end-result imagery goes.

3. **Get details. Who, What, Where, When and How Specifically?**

At this point, when you have a positive behavior, get all the details you can. You want to know Who, What, When, Where, Why and How. You want to know what they will see, hear and feel. We are not concerned with why. If they give you whys, you can make note, but we don't need to ask. When you feel like you have enough information to "tell them a story" of their future and lead them through detailed imagery of this behavior, move on to the next behavior. Ideally, you want about three good example behaviors to use during the hypnosis session.

Let's run through a quick example that will help you easily grasp this concept. In it, the subject (S) has come to the hypnotherapist (H) to quit smoking. In this example, the hypnotist has already done the pre-talk and suggestibility tests and will begin the induction as soon as the end-result interview is done. The interview is framed so that the subject has <u>already</u> succeeded and that all these questions are not about possibilities (would, could), but about definite certainties (will, can) - a very important part of end-result imagery.

Hynotist: "So, you're going to become a non-smoker. Great choice! Let me ask you, what will you be doing once you become a non-smoker?"

Subject: "Well, I won't be so antsy anymore."

["Won't" is negative. Let's get them to reframe this positively.]

H: "Great, so if you're <u>not</u> antsy, what <u>will</u> you be?"

S: "I guess... I'd be more calm."

[Now, calm is a state. And it's a nice state, but it's not a behavior. So, we will use question #1 to get a behavior.]

H: "Good, what will you be doing when you're more calm?"

S: "Relaxing!"

[Relaxing is the state of being relaxed. So, we'll plug "relaxing," into question #1 and keep asking for a behavior.]

H: "I'll bet! What kinds of things do you think you'll be doing when you're relaxing?"

S: "Hmm... Well, I'd be able to sit through a whole movie without having to get up and smoke a cigarette!"

[Bingo! Now we have a behavior. So we move on to question #3 and expand. We want details. Write everything down. Try to get as much of "Who, what, when, where and how" as possible.]

> **H:** "Wow. That <u>will</u> be nice! <u>Where</u> is it that you like to watch movies?"
>
> **S:** "I like that new Cineplex over on Crown Valley... with the stadium seats."
>
> **H:** "Oh yeah, those are nice seats. I'll bet you have someone that you like to go to the movies with too. <u>Who</u> do you like to go with?"
>
> **S:** "Yeah, my brother. We like Van Dam, Jackie Chan, Schwartzenegger. Action stuff... You know."

[We got both who and what on that answer.]

> **H:** "Yeah, I love that stuff. Do you get snacks and drinks and stuff?"
>
> **S:** "Yeah, we always get the big tub of popcorn."

[Some how]

These questions are interspersed in fluff talk so that the interview doesn't feel like 20 questions and get uncomfortable.

Ideally, we would want at least three behaviors for End-Result Imagery, so when you've got enough detail on this behavior, you ask again. "So, what <u>else</u> will you be doing when you _____?"

Now, once you've hypnotized your subject and done the convincers, you'll read back their End-Result Imagery. Here's an example of how it would sound based on the answers in the previous example:

"And I'd like you to *begin to imagine... Imagine a time in the future...* You and your brother are hanging out at the Cineplex. Just like the good-old times... But something is different this time... *Something...* Yes, *you're a non-smoker now...* You and your brother grab some popcorn and a couple of drinks and head in to watch the new action movie. Sitting there, in the dark, watching the movie, you begin to realize that *you feel wonderful* and *the urge to smoke is all gone... Now.* It feels great to know that you <u>can</u> sit there, in those big comfortable stadium seats... You can sit through that entire movie. And you can stay inside through the whole movie because *you're a non-smoker now.* Just *allow yourself to experience that* for a moment."

As you can see, end-result imagery creates powerful, customized imagery for the subject. This level of future pacing is a great way to install the subject's new, resourceful strategies, as well as providing an important "test" of their new behaviors before they leave your office.

Should I Work With Everything?

For the beginning hypnotist, there is an overwhelming desire to go out and "cure the world." Hypnosis is an amazingly powerful tool. It has helped people with everything from nail biting to bedwetting, depression to cancer. There are many issues to consider when performing hypnotherapy. There are moral, ethical and legal concerns.

The largest concern is the ecology of the patient. You must be sure that your suggestions are **safe**. It's fairly obvious that a sane person will reject a suggestion stating, "you can fly." However, a simple, harmless sounding suggestion such as, "you will eat less," can be interpreted very literally by the subconscious and may produce symptoms such as extreme as anorexia in some clients. Your suggestions need to be formed and delivered in the most direct way so as not to leave room for interpretation.

Another great concern is that, symptoms that seem easy to cure using hypnosis could be hiding a much more serious illness. For instance, the most extreme cases of nail biting could be a symptom of self-mutilation, which should obviously be treated by a qualified and licensed psychotherapist. If you take away the nail biting, the self-mutilation could manifest itself as hair pulling, cutting, or something worse. If a body builder comes to you and says his muscles hurt, you might feel inclined to take away that pain, until he lifts too much one day and tears a muscle. Sometimes pain is simply a nuisance, but sometimes it's a warning that lets us know our limits.

As you can see, learning what to work with and what not to work with is a balancing act and something you should think about before committing to work with anyone.

I provide the table on the following page only as a general guideline, and it is not to be taken as direct professional and/or legal advice. Neither the author nor the publisher can be held responsible for any actions taken as a result of reading this book or this chart. If you are a licensed mental health specialist, doctor, dentist, or any other licensed practitioner, this guideline may not apply to you. In your case, you know your scope of practice much better than I do, so use your own best judgment.

Safe	Gray Area	Needs Referral
Self Improvement Relaxation Improve Study Habits Test Anxiety Smoking Weight Self Hypnosis Increase Focus Sports Performance	Exercise Past-Life Regression Age Regression	Diagnosed illnesses Insomnia Depression Allergies Drug Addiction Alcohol Addiction Sexual Problems

Table 3.1 – Should I Work With Everything? (Adapted from information obtained through the International Board of Coaches and Practitioners, www.ibcponline.com)

In cases such as overcoming fears, improving self-esteem, bettering study habits, etc., you are usually perfectly safe doing hypnosis. For the more serious category, the most important rule to remember is this: First, I suggest making sure you are a certified hypnotherapist, then ask if they have seen a physician, therapist, counselor or whatever is appropriate for their symptoms. If they have not, send them on their way and ask them to come back once they have. If they have seen someone, give them a blank referral form and have them get you a referral from the person treating them. Then, WAIT until you have a referral from them. In many cases, it is the law, so heed this rule. And, make sure you are certified and competent before taking them on as a client.

Referral forms, admission forms and other necessary forms are available to students of our hypnotherapy courses. If you're interested in practicing clinical hypnotherapy, come and get certified. We teach the same course that got my career in hypnotherapy started. Visit **www.LearnHypnosisLive.com** for more information.

Overview - Read This

Whew... You've learned a lot in this chapter. If it seems overwhelming, it should. After all, if you choose to become a hypnotherapist, you'll be dealing with people's subconscious minds. This is a subject that should not be taken lightly.

At this point, you may feel like you're ready to go out, open your own practice and start healing people. Granted, you've learned a lot, but in my opinion, it would be extremely irresponsible to start a actual practice helping others without at least getting some hands-on training and getting certified. This book has given you a great head start and you'll likely breeze through the training, learning many new things along the way. There are many places to conduct your training, including Transform Destiny and other institutes approved by the International Board of Coaches and Practitioners.

I hope you have enjoyed this chapter and have learned a lot in the process. Now that you've learned how to use hypnosis to help others, be sure to check out Chapter 4 to learn how to use it to help **yourself**, using self-hypnosis in every aspect of your life.

Where to Learn More

If you wish to learn more about hypnosis, hypnotherapy, Neuro-Linguistic Programming, influence and persuasion or the subconscious mind in general visit the following websites:

Three-Day Hypnotherapy Certification Training:
www.LearnHypnosisLive.com

Live and Online NLP Courses and Trainings:
www.TransformDestiny.com

Ethical Influence and Persuasion:
www.InfluenceToProfit.com

Chapter 4: Self-Hypnosis

Overview

Even though the term, "Self-Hypnosis," is a bit redundant (since all hypnosis is self-hypnosis), it can be one of the most beneficial things you can do in your everyday life. It's easy to learn, feels great, and it's good for you too! Here you'll learn about how you can use hypnosis in your everyday life.

How Can It Help You?

Self-Hypnosis can be used to relieve stress, rid yourself of unwanted habits, work on higher self-esteem, improve your memory, gain better rapport with your subconscious mind, take a short rest (it's better than a power nap!), and many, many more things. The possibilities are limitless.

For instance, I have hypnotized myself to quit speeding on the freeway, to have better memory, to use my NLP skills subconsciously in my everyday life, and to eliminate limiting beliefs. These are just some of the big ones... There are many, many more, because I hypnotize myself every single day, for at least fifteen minutes a day.

How to Use Self-Hypnosis

Self-hypnosis, sometimes called *Auto-hypnosis,* is just like regular hypnosis, except that you lead **yourself** into trance. You'll also convince yourself and give yourself suggestions. When you're done, you'll also count yourself up.

So, how do you do it? It's easy! You already know how, because you read the first part of this book.

First, pick a place where you won't be disturbed by anything such as children, dogs, the television, or the phone. As you get better, you'll be able to do it in less peaceful situations, but for now, find a nice quiet place where you can relax.

It's best to pick a place where you can sit that has ample support from armrests to ensure that you won't fall out of the chair. While falling down during self-hypnosis is rare, you might as well be as safe as possible, this first time. A couch is a <u>great</u> place to sit.

Types of Inductions

Self Relaxation + Staircase

My favorite is the self-relaxation induction, because it can be done anywhere, almost instantly. For this induction, you'll pick one very simple suggestion, stated positively. For example, "Every day, I am moving toward my ideal weight," or the classic, "Every day, in every way, I'm feeling better and better."

This form of self-induction essentially follows the first progressive relaxation script I gave you back in Chapter 2. Simply relax every muscle, every nerve and every fiber of your body, starting from the crown of your head to the tips of your toes.

You can do this a variety of ways. You could imagine the same scene that you visualized when you listened to the sample MP3 in Chapter 1.

Or you could step through each area of your body as a rubber balloon, as each section blows up really big, and then totally deflates in a rush of air as the muscles relax.

Or you could imagine your body as thousands of tight rubber bands, as each body part just lets go, and the rubber bands get loose & floppy. The possibilities are endless!

My favorite relaxation is to tighten every muscle of my body for about five seconds, then I let go. And I mean really let go, so I slump down, as if someone had just cut the strings on a puppet.

Next, imagine yourself walking down the staircase with 10 stairs... relaxing your mind with each step... and at the bottom is pure relaxation: deep, deep hypnosis.

Next, do a convincer on yourself, as you learned in Chapter 3. After all, you need to be convinced, too, when you're the subject! I like to do heavy eyes, because it's the simplest.

Finally, repeat your suggestion to yourself, like a chant. You can choose to do it as many or as few times as you like, but I would suggest at least 10 repetitions.

The trick is to keep your suggestions short and sweet so that they can be repeated many times without much conscious effort.

When you're finished, it's time to come back to wakeful awareness. You can walk back up the stairway, or you can count yourself back up. I wouldn't suggest that you drift off to sleep at the end, as that might develop into a habit that could be hard to break.

Pre-Recorded Inductions

The next type of self-hypnosis induction is hypnosis recordings. These tapes, compact discs, and mp3's can be found in new-age stores, stage-hypnosis shows, and on the web at sites, such as mine at www.tranceout.com.

I actually got my start in hypnosis because of a tape I bought at the county fair. Some are good, some not so good. If you want to buy such inductions, my advice is that you buy them from www.tranceout.com, or from someone else you know and trust. That way you know you're getting a quality product.

Self-Recorded Induction

Guess what? <u>You</u> are a hypnotist now! With a voice recorder and a little creativity, you can actually record <u>your own</u> pre-recorded sessions! All you need is a basic voice recorder like one on your smart phone for a quick raw session, or a computer with an audio editing program to record a beautiful session complete with digital background music.

Using your computer may require extra software to record your own session and optionally burn it to CD. There is a program I highly recommend called *Audacity* which works on Windows, Macintosh and Linux. It is community developed – rather than being made by a corporation – so it's free. You can download it at http://audacity.sourceforge.net

You can learn how to use this free software and get my hypnotic background music included (normally $18.99) for free in my online course, "How To Create Hypnosis Recordings" at: www.LearnHypnosisNow.com/create-hypnosis-recordings

When Not to Use Self-Hypnosis

Since self-hypnosis is, essentially, focusing your attention inward, there are certain places that you should not use it.

Do not use self-hypnosis while driving, operating machinery of any kind, watching over someone who is immediately dependent on your attention or care, etc. Use common sense.

Self-hypnosis should only be used at times when you can sit quietly by yourself. Self-hypnosis is not an replacement for traditional medicine.

Chapter 5: Stage Hypnosis

Overview

Ok, we've all seen a stage hypnosis show, right? If not, find one and go see it. Stage hypnosis shows can be some of the most entertaining and mind-boggling shows you've ever seen.

What makes them so great? The fact that everyday people, like you and me, are called up on stage to do some of the most outrageously funny and totally baffling things you've ever seen. Seemingly normal people are "caused" to do utterly un-normal things. Because of this, many people think that stage hypnotism is fake. They couldn't be farther from the truth. Stage hypnosis is very real and a lot of fun if it's done right.

In this chapter, I'll tell you the four big secrets that will make any stage show practically run its self. We'll also explain the rapid induction and give you some great ideas for routines that you can use on stage.

This chapter is not meant to make you an expert stage-hypnotist. It is merely a starting point. To read some great books that focus on stage-hypnotism, read the Bibliography in Appendix IV.

OK, So What's the Secret?

You may have been one of those people who previously thought that hypnosis shows are all fake, right? At one point, I thought the same. There are four big secrets that make stage hypnosis work:

Volunteers: Always pick volunteers who are the most enthusiastic about coming on stage. These will be the "hams" in the audience. The ones most likely to perform for you – hypnotized or not. After all, the point of the show is not necessarily to hypnotize people, but rather to entertain the audience. Work with a large crowd and pick many enthusiastic volunteers.

Attitude: Never make hypnosis a challenge, or you will attract nay-sayers who will do everything in their power to resist. Instead, frame it as a series of experiments, and if they succeed, everyone will have fun. This puts them into a frame of mind where they will strive to do well to meet the expectations of you, their fellow volunteers, and the audience.

Paring down volunteers: Excuse volunteers back to their seat at the first sign of loss of trance or any kind of mischief. It is important to delicately handle the egos of these volunteers. After all, you're performing to entertain, not to make anybody feel bad. This can be easy easily accomplished by saying something like, "Sir/Miss, I think you will enjoy this show better from your own seat. Thank you... Let's give him/her a big hand..."

"As-if" principle: Structure your suggestions using the As-if principle and they will be more readily followed. For example, instead of saying, "When I count to three, your feet will be stuck to the floor." say, "When I count to three, you will feel *as if* your feet are stuck to the floor." This is much easier to follow, because even if they don't accept the suggestion that their feet will feel "stuck," they will still have the suggestion to act "as if" they were stuck.

How Do They Do It So Fast?

After reading most of this book, and experimenting with your new knowledge on friends and family, you may be wondering how stage hypnotists can get a whole group of people deep enough into trance to do all these crazy things in a matter of just a few minutes. After all, the induction you've learned in this book is long and drawn out, involving relaxation and imagery. While those types of inductions work well in therapy, they would make for a very long, boring show.

The answer is the *rapid induction*. Rapid inductions work extremely well for stage-hypnosis, and are based on the exaggeration of the five important principals of a successful induction:

Authority/Prestige: It is imperative that you demonstrate your authority in the area of hypnosis. Proper display of authority will create prestige, which will bring expectancy and rapport with it.

Rapport: Rapport and, more importantly, trust is key to your volunteers' acquiescence.

Expectation: Your volunteers' expectation of what is about to happen will be one of the largest factors for them going into trance. In some cases, when the expectation is great enough, all that is needed is a yank on the arm and a loud "SLEEP!" to do the trick.

Contract: Under most circumstances, a sort of a verbal contract is important for rapport in hypnosis. For example, "Is it OK if I hypnotize you now?" In the case of stage hypnotism, volunteering makes for a strong contract.

Even <u>with</u> this contract, it is safe to ask the group as a whole if it's OK to proceed after sufficient explanation of hypnosis.

Desire: Most of your volunteers will already have this. They <u>are</u> volunteers, after all!

With these five principles in place, you can speed up the induction to two- to four minutes and get great results.

Stage Ideas

A full break down of a stage-hypnosis show is well beyond the scope of this book, but I've included a few ideas that you can use to get you started once your subjects are in trance. Bear in mind that you will usually not know the names of your subjects. In order to address them with their eyes closed, it is necessary to place your hand on their head/shoulder/arm/leg and say something like, "you, who I'm touching..." Also, most of these "experiments" require you to wake your volunteer up to carry out the suggestion, so be sure to implant a *post-hypnotic* suggestion to go back into trance on command, once it's done.

Cannot stand/sit:

"You who I'm touching: On the count of three, when I will wake you up, you'll be surprised to find out that you can't sit down! No matter what you do, you have lost the ability to sit down. 1, 2, 3, WIDE AWAKE!"

Forgot the number 4:

"In a moment, when I wake you up, you will completely forget the number 4. It will just vanish from your mind completely. It will be as if the number four was never there. One, two, three, wide awake. How are you feeling?"

Subject: "Good."

Hypnotist: "Excellent. Sir, can you tell me how many fingers you have?"

S: "Ten."

H: "Ten, that's right. Can you do me a favor and count them?"

S: "Sure. 1-2-3-5-6-7-8-9-10-??-uh- eleven?"

H: "That doesn't sound right! Try it again."

S: "1-2-3-5-6-7-8.... (puzzled) I don't get it... I <u>used</u> to have 10..."

H: "I have an idea... Let's try this. What's seven minus three?"

S: "(Perplexed) uhh..."

H: "Very good... SLEEP!"

X-Ray Spyglass:

[This experiment requires a piece of cardboard cutout in the shape of a magnifying glass about 2 1/2 to 3 feet long.]

"When I awaken you, you'll notice an object in your lap. This object is an X-Ray Spy Glass capable of seeing right through everyone's clothes but mine! You will be able to see through everybody's clothes but mine when you look through this X-Ray Spy Glass, however, if I catch you using the spyglass, I will take it away, so be sure to hide it from me if I turn around to look your way. Again, I will take the spyglass away from you if I catch you using it, so be sure to hide it when I'm looking."

There are many other great skits and scenarios. See the Bibliography for other books specifically on Stage Hypnosis and hypnosis for entertainment.

Appendix I: The History of Hypnosis

Hypnosis spans back as far as written time in one form or another. Ancient Egyptians used sleeping temples in order to revitalize their spirits. Buddhists have been using mediation - a phenomenon very similar to hypnosis - for millennia.

Modern Hypnosis, however, began in the 18th century with a man named Franz Anton Mesmer. It was curiously tied to magnetism, which still has a following today.

Old School

Franz Anton Mesmer (1734 - 1815)

Franz Mesmer was a physician and a graduate of the famed Medical School of Vienna in 1776. After studying with a Jesuit priest, Mesmer became interested in magnetism. Magnetism was a holistic medical practice where magnets were passed over the bodies of patients to promote healing. The results were fabulous and Mesmer became Europe's foremost expert.

Mesmer believed that each living being had an invisible magnetic "fluid" that ran throughout their body. It was his theory that a person with enough of this magnetic fluid would be strong and healthy. If a person had a lack of magnetic fluid, he would become very ill and possibly die.

This was termed "Animal Magnetism," coining the popular phrase.

Mesmer routinely practiced his magnetism, becoming very famous. One day, while tending to a patient, he discovered that he did not have his magnets. Wanting to perform, Mesmer went through the motions without his magnets, not expecting his session to be successful, but to Mesmer's surprise, the patient was relieved of his ailment. Mesmer declared that he no longer needed the magnets for he had enough of the fluid within him that he could administer the healings himself! This, along with his claim that women need not suffer pain during childbirth, caused a terrible blow to his reputation. He moved from Vienna to Paris in 1778 to escape constant reticule.

Mesmer grew to immense popularity while in Paris. Everyone who was anyone went to see him for sessions and he became one of the elite. He also became over-confidant. He insisted that King Louis XVI establish a panel to prove the reality of his practice and quiet his detractors. This was a grave mistake.

To achieve this, he make the bold claim that he had discovered the "fifth element," his invisible magneticfluid. The king ordered the Royal Academie of Science in Paris to investigate.

A panel of noteworthy men were commissioned at the order of the King. Antoine-Laurent de Jessieu, a famous botanist, Dr. Guillotin, inventor of the guillotine, Antoine-Laurent Lavosier, a chemist, and Benjamin Franklin, serving as an American Ambassador in France, were set to the task. They studied Mesmer for weeks in awe of his ability to heal, but could not find a "fifth element."

Benjamin Franklin spoke for the commission when he wrote "This fellow Mesmer is not flowing anything from his hands that I can see. Therefore, this Mesmerism must be a fraud." His reputation ruined, Franz Mesmer died a poor and lonely man in Germany in 1815.

Some time later, Marquis de Pusseguyr continued the study of Mesmer's work and later coined the term *somnambulism*, which we still use today to describe a deep state of hypnosis.

To this day, the term "mesmerized," derived from Mesmer's name, is used to describe someone in a captivated trance.

James Braid (1795 – 1860)

A surgeon in Manchester, England, James Braid was the first person to accurately describe hypnosis as more than magnetism.

In 1841, he set out to discredit Mesmerism at a public demonstration by the traveling mesmerist, Lafontaine. Instead he became convinced of Lafontaine's young volunteer's deep trance. This fascinated Braid to no end and he began studying its usefulness in relation to surgery.

Hypnosis was originally called Neurypnology by Braid. It almost became Monoideaism, meaning to hold one idea, but luckily, neither name stuck. The word Hypnosis, also coined by Braid is Greek for, "nervous sleep."

In 1843, James Braid published the first book on Hypnotism, which gave it its name, titled "Neurypnology". His focus was on using hypnosis for pain-free surgery.

You can download this book for <u>free</u> at:

www.LearnHypnosisNow.com/Braid-Neurypnology

James Esdaile (1808 – 1859)

Before the discovery of Chloroform or other anesthesias for surgery, the mortality rate was alarming. Up to 80% of patients died during major surgery from fear or shock or infection. Not the most pleasing odds.

James Esdaile, a Scottish surgeon working in India, beat those odds hands down. Esdaile would spend up to two hours preparing a patient for surgery. Using eye fixation, sounds, and slow, sweeping motions Esdaile would put his patients into a deep hypnotic state, causing full anesthesia throughout the body. His mortality rate dropped from 80% to 10% - Something unheard of at that time.

Esdaile performed over 1000 operations using hypnosis as his only anesthesia, over 300 of them major surgeries, and 19 of them amputations before he was tried by the Medical Association of England, losing his medical license.

Liebault & Bernheim and the Nancy School for Hypnotism

Ambroise A. Liebault (1823 – 1904) was a French Physician living near Nancy, France. Commonly known as the "Father of Suggestive Hypnosis," Liebault moved to Nancy where he worked for free to avoid persecution from the detractors of mesmerism. As long as he didn't charge for his services, they could not call him a "quack". In 1866, he published the culmination of all his hard work titled "Du Sommeil". Only one copy was sold.

Leibault's work went largely unrecognized until he teamed up with Hippolyte Bernheim (1837 – 1919), a professor at the Nancy School of Medicine. Bernheim was a more logical and scientific man than his predecessors. He didn't make extravagant claims about hypnosis, but merely stated the facts. He published these facts in his work "Suggestive Therapeutics: A Treatise on the Nature and Uses of Hypnosis". They soon opened the Nancy School of Hypnosis where many of the future hypnotists of the world were trained. The building still stands today in Nancy, France.

Jean-Martin Charcot (1825 – 1893)

Charcot was a neurologist in Paris in the 1800's specializing in the study of neurological disorders. He is probably most famous for first documenting and studying hysteria, which later became known as Post Traumatic Stress Disorder, or PTSD.

His initial conclusions about hypnosis were not favorable. He believed that hypnosis was an abnormal behavior, and furthermore, was a state of hysteria. He was later discredited by Bernheim because of this belief and went to study with him at the Nancy School of Hypnosis.

Sigmund Freud (1856 – 1939)

The father of "Talk Therapy", Sigmund Freud, then a physician in Vienna, began taking an interest in hypnosis as it gained popularity and became more mainstream. He went to France to and was trained in hypnotism by Dr. Charcot at the Nancy School of Hypnosis. When Freud returned to Vienna, he began to practice hypnosis with his partner Dr. Breuer with great success.

Freud eventually publicly denounced hypnosis, a crushing blow that would destroy its reputation for years, when he claimed that a young lady suddenly jumped up and kissed him on the lips while in trance. The actual story is thought to be a little less exciting than all that.

Freud frequently used cocaine leaves between his cheeks and gums to control pain, a common practice at that time. This eventually led to the destruction of his gums, which caused his dentures to fit poorly. Because of this, Freud slurred and could not speak clearly enough to lead people into hypnosis. Regardless, his public "story" severely damaged the credibility of hypnosis in the medical field.

He later credited hypnosis for driving him in the right direction to create his methods. From his studies of hypnotism, he began to formulate his theories of "talk therapy" and the concept of modern Freudian psychology was born.

The New Fathers of Hypnosis

Hypnosis enjoyed a revived interest in the late 1940's and early 1950's. Approved as a valid treatment medium by the American Medical Association in 1958, physicians, dentists and therapists began, once again, to experiment with and study hypnosis.

Milton H. Erickson (1902 - 1984)

Born in Aurum, Nevada and raised in Wisconsin, Erickson became interested in hypnosis after witnessing a demonstration by Clark Hull. He was so impressed that he met with and hypnotized Hull after the show! He taught himself hypnosis from that point on.

Erickson had a great understanding of the human mind. While an MD and a Psychiatrist, he received his most important training at a younger age. He explains in this quote taken from "Dr. Erickson's Personality and Life" by Jay Haley - 1967:

"I had a polio attack when 17 years old and I lay in bed without a sense of body awareness. I couldn't even tell the position of my arms or legs in bed. So I spent hours trying to locate my hand or my foot or my toes by a sense of feeling, and I became, acutely aware of what movements were.

"Later, when I went into medicine, I learned the nature of muscles. I used that knowledge to develop an adequate use of the muscles polio had left me and to limp with the least possible strain; this took me ten years. I also became extremely aware of physical movements and this has been exceedingly useful. People use those little telltale movements, those, adjustive movements that are so revealing if one can notice them.

"So much of our communication is in our bodily movements, not in our speech. I've found that I can recognize a good piano player not by the noises he makes, but by the ways his fingers touch the keys. The sure touch, the delicate touch, the forceful touch that is so accurate. Proper playing involves such exquisite physical movement."

Milton H. Erickson essentially revolutionized the field of hypnosis. While there are those that promote and teach a pure Ericksonian technique, elements of Erickson's wisdom are present in almost every hypnotist's style these days. A proper discussion of Ericksonian techniques is truly beyond the scope of an introductory book (there are, in fact, many entire volumes written on the subject – Check the bibliography).

His style of conversational hypnosis would literally hypnotize people with their eyes open in everyday conversation. This is one of the powerful things that we teach in our NLP Practitioner Certification courses.

Dave Elman (1900 - 1967)

As a young boy, Dave Elman had to watch his father, a stage-hypnotist, dying a terribly painful death from cancer. A week before his father was to pass away, a friend of the family, also a hypnotist came and put his father into trance to take away his pain. Young Dave snuck into the room and watched in hiding as the hypnotist did his work. This was the last time the Dave Elman saw his father peaceful, playful and in good spirits. It made a lasting impression.

Elman spent the rest of his life dedicated to teaching hypnosis to licensed professionals. Doctors, psychologists, dentists, pediatricians and more flocked to his classes week after week as Elman traveled the country with his wife.

Elman specialized in a rapid induction that worked very well much of the time. This opened the door for medical applications where the doctor did not have the time to spend ten to twenty minutes inducing the patient into hypnosis. Word of mouth spread fast and Elman's class was a success. He wrote one book that describes it all before he passed away. In my opinion, it is a must read for anyone interested in professional hypnosis… medical or not. Check the bibliography for more information.

Elman's style of hypnosis is what we teach in our NLP Master Practitioner certification course.

Ormond McGill (1913 – 2005)

The Dean of Modern Stage Hypnosis, Ormond McGill has been described as "…one of the true giants in the history of hypnotism".

Beginning in the late 1920s, McGill developed a stage style that is unrivalled even today. Many of today's great hypnotists have gotten their start or honed their style at Ormond's seminar. His book, The Encyclopedia of Stage Hypnotism is a must read for anyone that aspires to perform stage hypnosis.

Richard Bandler and John Grinder

Bandler and Grinder are the co-founders of *NLP*, Neuro-Linguistic Programming. NLP is loosely related to hypnosis and is based, in part, on theories of "quick change" developed by Erickson in psychotherapy. NLP has become a favorite tool of many hypnotists because of its rapport building abilities and the ability to squash phobias and cause change quickly in the subject – even being able to help someone change covertly (without their conscious awareness that you're doing so).

Richard Bandler was a mathematics and computer science major studying at the University of San Jose in the early 70's. He became interested in psychotherapy while editing a book written by Dr. Virginia Satir and approached John Grinder, his linguistics professor and master of linguistics to propose a study of the structure of the language patterns that therapists use to cure patients. The combination of Bandler's structured logical thinking and propensity for experimentation and Grinder's breakdown of language was something that therapy had not seen before. By studying the *patterns* of noteworthy, successful therapists (Fritz Pearl, psychologist; Gregory Bateson, Linguistics/General Semantics; Virginia Satir, Family Therapy; Milton H. Erickson, hypnotist), they developed a set of "cookie cutter" techniques that anyone could use to cause change – even without psychology training.

NLP has also been applied to everything from persuasion to power writing to sales and marketing. There are many resources available in the Bibliography.

We teach NLP in many different topics in many of our live and online courses. Whether you want to become a certified practitioner or just use NLP in your life, business or relationships, we have courses that will be the perfect fit for what you are looking for. Visit a www.transformdestiny.com for more info on our products and trainings.

A.M. Krasner (1928 – 2013)

Founder of the American Board of Hypnotherapy (originally called the California Council of Hypnotherapy), Dr. Krasner has pioneered and taught many of the techniques used in modern hypnotherapy. His simple, no frills technique for putting the subject at ease (and then putting the subject into trance) is documented well in his book (see the Bibliography).

The first live hypnosis course I ever took was The Krasner Method of Hypnotherapy and Krasner significantly shaped my early notions and style of hypnotherapy.

Krasner changed the tone of hypnosis because he believed that everyone – not just licensed professionals should learn hypnosis. Dr Krasner's contribution was so great that he was selected for inclusion in the Directory of Distinguished Americans for outstanding contributions to the field of hypnotherapy.

<u>Appendix II: Glossary</u>

- Amnesia: Total forgetting of a specific event or subject.

- Anesthesia: Complete loss of sensation in a particular area of the body.

- Analgesia: Loss of pain sensation, but retention of pressure and heat sensations

- Auto-Hypnosis: Self-Hypnosis

- Catalepsy: A perfect balance of the opposing muscles in the area of the body, keeping an appendage or the whole body rigid.

- Cessation: The act of removing a habit, such as smoking cessation

- Congruence: Behaving in a way that is in line with the words that you speak.

- Direct Commands: Commands given to a subject in a direct manner, such as "stand up," or "you will quit smoking".

- Eye Fixation: Having the subject stare at a spot until the eyes become so tired that they close on their own.

- Fractionation: Bringing the subject out-of and back in-to trance repeatedly to deepen their trance.

- Glove Anesthesia: Anesthesia that begins in the hand and can be transferred to any part of the body through the hand.

- Intervention: The act of "curing" a person using suggestions and other modalities such as NLP.

- Metaphor: A short story tailored to the situation of the subject.

- NLP or Neuro Linguistic Programming: A modality for creating generative change in your subject using many techniques.

- Pace: Following your subject with your body language, movements, tonality, tempo, or choice of words.

- Pattern Interruption: A technique whereby the hypnotist can interrupt a common movement in the subject to rapidly induce trance.

- Post-Hypnotic Suggestion: Suggestions to be carried out after the subject has been awakened. Sometimes triggered by a specified event or word being spoken.

- Rapid Induction: An induction which utilizes the five traits of good suggestions to rapidly induce trance in a subject.

- Rapport: A feeling of comfort and trust shared between the hypnotist and the subject.

- Suggestion: Words formed in a way such that the subject feels compelled to act out the command.

- Tempo: The speed and rhythm of the words you speak.

- Tonality: The pitch, or relative high-ness or low-ness of your voice.

- Yes Sets: Stacking realities, where each portion of the yes set requires the subject to answer yes, so that a yes outcome for the desired part is more likely.

Appendix III: Scripts

These scripts are compiled here for your convenience. Some are mine and some are public domain scripts from the internet. For more scripts, check the bibliography.

Inductions

Here are a few of the more common inductions used today.

Relaxation Method I

"Turn loose now, relax. Let a good, pleasant feeling come all across your body. Let every muscle and every nerve grow so loose and so limp and so relaxed. Arms limp now, just like a rag doll. That's good.

"Now, send a pleasant wave of relaxation over your entire body, from the top of your head to the tips of your toes. Just let every muscle and nerve grow loose and limp and relaxed. You are feeling more relaxed with each easy breath that you take.

"Droopy, drowsy and sleepy. So calm and so relaxed. You're relaxing more with each easy beat of your heart ... with each easy breath that you take ... with each sound that you hear."

Relaxation Method II

"Your arms are loose and limp, just like a rag doll. As I raise your hand, just let all of the weight hang limply in my fingers. And when I drop it, send a wave of relaxation all across your body. As you feel you hand touch your body, send that wave of relaxation from the top of your head all the way down to the very tips of your toes.

"And as you do, you find that you double your previous level of relaxation.

"Now, once again, with the other hand."

[Repeat with other hand]

Staircase Method

"In a moment I'm going to relax you more completely. In a moment I'm going to begin counting backwards from 10 to 1.

"The moment I say the number 10 you will allow your eyelids to remain closed. The moment I say the number 10, you will, in your minds eye, see yourself at the top of a small set of stairs.

"The moment I say the number 9, and each additional number, you will simply move down those stairs relaxing more completely. At the base of the stairs is a large feather bed, with a comfortable feather pillow.

"The moment I say the number one you will simply sink into that bed, resting your head on that feather pillow.

Number 10, eyes closed at the top of those stairs. Ten ...

Nine, relaxing and letting go. Nine ...

Eight, sinking into a more comfortable, calm, peaceful position ...

Seven ....

Six ... going way down ...

Five ... moving down those stairs, relaxing more completely.

Four ...

Three ... breathe in deeply ...

Two ... On the next number, number one, simply sinking into that bed, becoming more calm, more peaceful, more relaxed ...

One ... Sinking into that feather bed, let every muscle go limp and loose as you sink into a more calm, peaceful state of relaxation."

Stiff Arm Method

"Raise and stiffen your arm. Make a fist."

[Help subject achieve this position, then let go]

"That's good. Just like a steel bar, stiff and powerful. So stiff and rigid and so powerful that the more you try to lower or bend your arm, the stiffer and tighter it becomes. Try to lower or bend your arm and find it locking stiff; stiff and rigid. The harder you try, the stiffer it becomes.

"That's fine. When I touch your forehead, your arm drops limply down and you go deeper in sleep."

[Tap forehead]

Arm-Drop Method

[The subject is asked to raise an arm so that the hand is slightly above the head and given suggestions. There are a number of aspects of this induction which are worthy of special notice. First, the arm is placed in such a position that fatigue will eventually bring it down. The downward movement is tied into going "down" into a "deep state of relaxation." The harder the individual keeps fighting to hold it up, the more he is committed to the proposition implied by the statement that, "You will not go into a deep state of relaxation until the arm is all the way down." This means, of course, that, "You will go into such a state when the arm comes all the way down."]

[Have subject raise arm so that hand is slightly above head]

"Stare at one of the fingers, either the index or the middle finger. You may continue to look at it, or, if you wish, close your eyes and visualize it in your mind's eye. As you fixate your gaze on it you will notice that the other fingers tend to fade out of focus and that your entire arm begins to feel heavier and heavier. The longer you concentrate on that finger the heavier and heavier your arm becomes. But you will not go into a deep state of relaxation until the arm has come all the way down. Keep concentrating on that finger while the arm gets heavier and heavier and heavier."

[When downward movement become apparent]

"Notice that as the arm is getting heavier it is slowly coming down, down, down. But you will not relax into a deep and profound state of relaxation until the arm is all the way down. Going down, down, down, deeper, deeper, deeper."

[Continue deepening comments: The suggestions must be timed with the actual movement of the arm]

Arm Levitation Method I

[This induction (or deepening) technique requires that the hypnotist gauge the pace of the suggestions to the response of the subject.]

"I'm going to count from one up to twenty. As I do, a light, easy, pleasant feeling moves into your right hand and into your right arm. As I continue counting, that feeling grows stronger and stronger. Soon you'll feel the first slight movement of your fingers, a twitching of the muscles."

[At this point, grasp the subjects arm and demonstrate how it will move as you continue with the following suggestions.]

"Then your hand begins to lift. Your arm begins to lift. It continues moving, lifting, and rising until it comes to rest upon your body.

"Now when you feel the movement in your hand and in your arm, don't try to resist. You could resist if you chose to, that is not why you are here. Just let your subconscious mind do its perfect work. All right, now we are ready to begin.

"Number One - The first light, easy sensation moves into the fingertips of your right hand.

"Number Two - The feeling is spreading around beneath the fingernails.

"Number Three - It is moving up to the first joint of the fingers.

"Number Four - Spreading to the large knuckle across the back of the hand.

"Number Five - the first slight movements begin to start taking place. Slight movements of the fingers, a twitching of the muscles.

"Number Six - The light sensation spreads all across the back of your hand.

"Number Seven - Spreading over and into your thumb.

"Number Eight - Moving now all through the palm of your hand.

"Number Nine - The light sensation spreads up and into your wrist. Think of your left hand now. You'll see by comparison, your left hand is beginning to feel very, very heavy.

"While on Number Ten your right hand grows lighter and lighter with each number I count; just as light as a feather floating in the breeze and even lighter. As light as a gas-filled balloon. Just as a gas-filled balloon will rise and float towards the ceiling, in the same way, by the time I reach the count of twenty, your right hand is moving, lifting, rising and floating.

"Number Eleven - The light sensation has moved beyond your wrist now, spreading into your forearm.

"Number Twelve, Thirteen - Once again, think of your left hand. Your left hand has grown so heavy, it feels as though it were made of marble or stone.

"Number Fourteen - That light sensation is spreading up toward your elbow.

"Now on Fifteen - From the fingertips all the way up to the elbow your hand has grown light, light and free. It's beginning to lift. It's moving, lifting, rising and floating."

[At this point, if the hand is not moving, gently lift the hand to get it started]

"All right, Sixteen - Now your arm is moving and lifting and rising. And as your arm is lifting, you're going deeper and deeper into hypnosis.

"Seventeen - Your hand continues moving, lifting and rising now until it comes to rest over on your body.

"Eighteen - Moving, lifting, rising, floating. Right on over now and when your hand comes to rest upon your body, at that time your eyelids lock tightly closed. Your eyelids lock so tightly closed at that point, the more you try to open them the tighter they're locking closed.

"Nineteen - Your hand is getting ready to come down and rest upon your body.

"Twenty - Now your hand has come to rest upon your body and at the same time, your eyelids are locked so tightly closed, the more you try to open your eyelids the tighter they are locking closed.

"That's fine, stop trying and go deeper into trance."

Confusion Method

The basic message to this induction is the conscious forgetting, and the subconscious knowing. This message is drawn out and repeated. Separate directions for the conscious mind, and separate directions for the subconscious mind. Maintain the subconscious attention, while dismissing the conscious attention both by the suggestions and the pauses and mental fatigue.

[Have the subject sit or lay in a relaxed position, with their eyes closed. Read the text slowly and rhythmically.]

"Just close your eyelids and let your mind drift where it will.

"You are aware of everything, and yet you are not aware. You are listening with your subconscious mind, while your conscious mind is far away, and not listening. Your conscious mind is far away, and not listening. Your subconscious mind is awake, and listening, and hearing everything while your conscious mind remains very relaxed and peaceful.

"You can relax peacefully because your subconscious mind is taking charge, and when this happens, you close your eyes and let your subconscious do all the listening. Your subconscious mind knows, and because your subconscious mind knows, your conscious mind does not need to know and can stay asleep, and not mind while your subconscious mind stays wide awake.

"You have much potential in your subconscious mind which you don't have in your conscious mind. You can remember everything that has happened with you subconscious mind, but you cannot remember everything with your conscious mind. You can forget so easily, and with forgetting certain things you can remember other things. Remembering what you need to remember, and forgetting what you can forget.

"It does not matter if you forget, you need not remember. Your subconscious mind remembers everything that you need to know and you can let your subconscious mind listen and remember while your conscious mind sleeps and forgets. Keep your eyes closed, and listen with your subconscious mind, and when you're listening very, very carefully, your head can now "yes".

"As you continue to listen to me, with your subconscious mind, your conscious mind sleeps deeper and deeper, and deeper, and deeper. Let your conscious mind stay deeply asleep, and let your subconscious mind listen to me."

[Repeat beginning with the second sentence since their eyelids are already closed. Use a deepening technique and test subject]

Forest and Stream Method

[For this induction it is helpful to have background sounds of water, birds, and other forest sounds, but do not start the sounds until indicated in the induction]

"To prepare yourself for this enjoyable, helpful experience, be sure you have all tight clothes loosened, and then get yourself in just as comfortable a position as you can ...

"Now close your eyes and inhale deeply and hold it for three or four seconds and then exhale slowly ... (Pause as subject responds)

"Again breathe in deeply and exhale slowly ... keep doing that 5 or 6 more times ...

"As you inhale, you bring more oxygen into your body, and as you exhale it causes your body to keep relaxing more and more ... (Pause and observe)

"Now you can continue breathing easily and freely, and can feel yourself becoming more calm and peaceful ...

"You are revealing signs that indicate you are moving into a very deep, peaceful state of relaxation ... as I continue talking to you, you can keep relaxing more peacefully ... not caring how deeply you relax, just happy to continue becoming more calm, more peaceful, and more at ease ... continuing to breathe easily and freely ...

"Your subconscious mind will always be aware of what I'm saying to you, so it keeps becoming less and less important for you to consciously listen to my voice ...

"Your subconscious mind, and all levels of your inner mind can hear and receive everything I tell you, and your conscious mind can relax completely ...

"You are continuing to experience perfect peace of mind, and can feel yourself moving into the situation I describe to you ... it's going to happen automatically, and you don't even need to think about it consciously ..."

[Optional: Start background tape of birds and water. Pause about 30 seconds after starting background sounds]

"Now I want you to imagine yourself lying in a comfortable position near a stream of fresh, clear water, in a beautiful forest on a perfect summer day...

"There is a warm, gentle breeze, and the air is fresh and clean, the sound of the peaceful stream is very relaxing...

"It keeps becoming less important for you to consciously listen to my voice because your subconscious mind and all levels of your inner mind are hearing and receiving everything I say...

"In your mind, you are enjoying the beauty of nature, as the sunlight shines through the trees and you listen to the gentle flow of water and the birds singing cheerfully...

"You are lying there, comfortably relaxing ... it is so peaceful that you continue feeling more relaxed than ever before in your entire life...

"As you continue enjoying this peaceful, pleasant experience, a soothing drowsiness is coming over your whole body, from the top of your head to the bottom of your feet...

"You continue feeling calmer, more relaxed and more secure...

"And now, as you lie there with your eyes closed, you are so relaxed and comfortable and happy that you continue moving into a more peaceful, more detached state...

"It may seem like you are drifting into a state of sleep...

"There may be times when it seems like my voice is a long distance away... and there may be times, when I'm talking to you, that you will not be consciously aware of my voice, and that's okay, because your subconscious mind is still receiving every word I say, and is making true everything I tell you...

"From now on you will be influenced only by positive thoughts, ideas and feelings...

"The following thoughts come to you... I am calm, secure, and relaxed... I am comfortable and at ease... I am in control of myself at all times ... I am responsible for my body, and will always treat my body well ... my mind enables me to be relaxed and calm as I go about the activities of my daily life..."

[Note: The following paragraphs can be used for therapy]

"Your subconscious mind, and all levels of your inner mind can now review and examine what has caused that problem, and can assess that information and work out a solution that is pleasing to you...

"And you will be pleased to notice yourself improving more each day, and you can be sure it is permanent and lasting...

"When your inner mind understands what has caused that problem and realizes that it is okay for you to get rid of that problem, one of the fingers on your right hand will lift up towards the ceiling and will remain up until I tell it to go back down."

[Note: as the subject's mind is reviewing the information and you are waiting for finger to lift, give suggestions from an appropriate prescription pertaining to the problem]

Hand to Face Method

[Tell subject to get as comfortable as possible with their arms resting on the arms of the chair. Show subject how you would like them to hold their hand in front of their face. Palm of their hand facing in towards their face, with fingers pointing upward pressed lightly together. Hand should be about eye level. Have subject close their eyes and begin with progressive relaxation and then proceed with the Hand To Face induction.]

"In just a moment, when I ask you to, I am going to have you bring one of your hands up in front of your face, fingers extended upwards and pressed together. I am then going to have you try to open your eyes, and pick a spot on your hand. It may seem difficult to open the eyes, and keep them open, which is only natural since you have been relaxing so far. I am going to want you to try, and open your eyes, and with a little effort you will at least be able to get them open.

"Now, the one thing that you must accomplish is that I want you to remain totally relaxed, and at ease even with your eyes open, and your hand in this position.

"Remaining relaxed, and at ease, move your hand up in front of your face with the fingers pointed upward, and pressed together.

"Now, attempt to open your eyes, and pick one spot on your hand, and begin to concentrate on it.

"As you concentrate on that one spot, and one spot only, your fingers are going to spread apart.

"You do not have to make them spread, but do not try and stop them ... concentrate, and allow things to take place.

"Feel them spreading apart now. Automatically separating now ... It is beginning to feel as though there was a string tied to each finger pulling them apart. Separating further, and further."

[Once the fingers have separated, proceed in the following way]

"Now, please do not let it disturb you that the drowsy, heavy feeling in your eyes is becoming stronger now that your fingers have spread apart.

"It is a very normal, natural sensation. As I begin to count from 5 down to 1 that heavy, drowsy feeling will continue to grow stronger."

[Continue with deepening technique]

Ink Spot Induction – Three to Six Years of Age

[This technique requires a bottle of ink. I prefer a bottle of disappearing ink that can be bought at any local magic store or gift store that sells gag magic. The disappearance of the ink can be worked into the script very convincingly.

Seat the child in a chair and put his dominant hand in his lap, palm down. Place a drop of the ink on the back of that hand, and then begin.]

"Look at that ink spot, there on the back of the hand. What do you suppose it means?

"Look hard at it, because, in a moment, it's going to begin to slowly rise. It will come up and come closer and closer to your forehead. As it does, you may notice the ink disappearing, and that means you're going into a far away pretend place where you can close your eyes and go there, and have some fun.

"The harder you try to look away from the ink spot, the faster and faster it will move toward your face. And when you feel that hand touching your face, you'll close your eyes and go to that special place, and your neck will become relaxed, and your head will become very heavy and tired."

[From time to time, you may need to encourage the arm to move with a slight touch to get it started, only if there is no movement after a minute or so. Once the child closes their eyes and relaxes, reassure them that they will feel fine and rest, and when they're done, you'll have a special surprise gift waiting for them.]

Toy Soldier Induction – Six to Twelve Years of Age

[To begin this technique, have the child stand completely up against the wall, with their heels, bottom, back, shoulders and head all touching the wall. Bring up a chair and sit in the chair, about a foot to a foot-and-a-half in front of the child.]

"Now, in a few seconds, I'm going to count from one to three. And when I get to three, I want you to pretend you are a wooden soldier... You know the kind. Pretend your body is made from one solid piece of wood, and I want you to try to bend at the waist. And I mean really try. And the harder you try to bend, the more rigid and stiff your back will become. Even though you know you can't bend, I want you to keep trying. You'll bend so hard, you'll fall into my arms and fall deeply asleep, but your "other mind" will still be listening. One, two, three!"

Hole In The Top Of The Head Induction – Five Years of Age and Up

[This is a fun induction and works very quickly to induce a light trance in children, but can also be used with adults as a suggestibility test or a way to give a few quick suggestions. Begin lightly tapping on the middle of the top of the client's head.]

"I want you to imagine there's a hole in the top of your head, right here were I'm tapping.

"Go ahead and close your eyes and begin looking through that hole on the top of your head. Look through that hole so you can see the ceiling. Keep looking through that hole, no matter what you do.

"When I count to three, your eyelids will be shut tight. They'll be locked tight so that you just can't open them. It will be funny, and when they stay locked tight, something magical will happen, and I want you to imagine that your living in your favorite TV show, during your favorite episode.

"One… two… three - [*snap*]

"Try to open your eyes and notice how funny it is that they're locked. And now you're in your favorite TV show, living your favorite episode, easily and effortlessly. And I'll expect you to tell me all about it when we're done."

[Once you're done giving suggestions, bring them back]

"Ok, now, in a second, I'm going to count from one to three, and then I'll clap my hands. When I do, you'll find that you can open your eyes, and you'll open them and tell me all about your adventure on your favorite TV show. One... two... three - [*clap*]"

Interventions

Here are a few of the more common interventions encountered today. See the Bibliography for information on other books that focus solely on scripts.

Anger / Temper

"See yourself in a situation where you might have lost your temper in the past. This time see yourself in control You no longer respond with anger. You respond with understanding and are calm. You no longer fee a need to retaliate.

"You can now allow people to be themselves and allow them their own priorities. You no longer get angry because they do not agree with you. The only value someone else's opinion has, is the value you give it. You no longer get angry because their opinion is different from yours. You are in control of your own emotions and reacting with anger is negative. You are now choosing to be positive. You will never again react with uncontrolled anger.

"Instead of becoming angry, you can now see their view. You now react with understanding and care and are calm. You react with positive thoughts and emotions."

[Find what triggers anger most and have client visualize a similar situation while maintaining a calmness.]

Finding Internal Resources: The Castle

"As you go even deeper now, I want you to imagine yourself on a wonderfully natural, perfectly green pathway. It's incredibly peaceful and tranquil. All the shades of green are vibrant and alive.

"As you look around feeling the breeze on your skin you notice that all of your favorite flowers are growing next and pathway. The breeze begins carrying the sweet smell of these flowers to your nose as the sun warms your skin. You feel incredible sense of calm coming over you.

"As you begin to walk down this pathway now, feeling as peaceful and tranquil as can be, you notice all the beauty and wonder of this amazing place. As you round a corner, the pathway opens up into a large clearing.

"In the middle of the clearing is a large, strong, majestic looking castle. This castle somehow seems very familiar, as you realize this is your castle. You make your way closer as the sound of the flags flapping in the light breeze takes your attention. And as you make your way toward the gate, the drawbridge lowers you enter with a sense of familiarity, confidence and security.

"Inside the castle, you look around and notice the surroundings. You realize that you haven't been here very long time. It's very dirty, and a musty smell fills the air. You decide that it's time to clean up, inside.

"The day is hot and the work is hard, and you find yourself getting thirstier and thirstier for some clear cool water. As you scrub, rinse and clean inside the castle, it gets warmer and warmer, and you get thirstier and thirstier.

"You come upon an amazing room filled with treasures of all kinds. This is the storehouse of all the vast, untapped resources, inside. All the potential for good, and all the resources for achievement which you have not yet tapped into are stored in this room.

"All of these treasures are rightfully yours, for they have been stored here by you, for you, whenever you want and need them.

"Naturally, you want this treasure, because it's rightfully yours. Yet, you cannot take it.

"Some force is preventing you from taking the treasure. The force is emanating from a huge black statue in the center of the room. The statue, powered by a magnificent jewel embedded within its forehead, and is the embodiment of all of the negative forces of failure and defeat within you. It's been placed in this room as the guardian of treasures, making all other guardians unnecessary.

"To free this incredible storehouse of untapped potential so that you can become the person you're capable of being, you must first overcome the negative forces of failure and defeat within you which are acting to prevent this. These tendencies are personified and embodied within that massive statue.

"Go to the statue and knock the jewel free from its forehead. As it falls to the ground, notice that it loses its shine. There on the floor, it continues changing to what looks like the lump of coal, and you can step on it with your foot and crush it. Now that the power of the statue is gone, you can push the statue over and watch as it shatters into a thousand pieces on the ground.

"You're now free to gather up any and all of the treasure you so desire from the storehouse. You can take these treasures back with you as you retrace your steps to the drawbridge.

"There's no need to take all of the treasure, because it is rightfully yours and you can come back anytime that you so desire. No matter how much treasure you take, the room will never be empty. It will always be filled with new treasures only for you.

"Any time you feel a lack of confidence in your ability to have, be, and do what you want, think of your castle and all of the treasures contained within. As you do, you'll feel a great sense of strength, power and confidence surging through you, filling you with the certainty you are capable of doing anything that you want and accomplishing any task about which you thought you were doubtful."

Grieving a Loved One

"As you go even deeper now, I want you to imagine yourself on a wonderfully natural, perfectly green pathway. It's incredibly peaceful and tranquil. All the shades of green are vibrant and alive. You're carrying a small satchel over your shoulder and enjoying the scenery.

"As you look around feeling the breeze on your skin you notice that all of your favorite flowers are growing next and pathway. The breeze begins carrying the sweet smell of these flowers to your nose as the sun warms your skin. You feel incredible sense of calm coming over you.

"As you make your way to the top of a small hill, you notice a majestic gate spanning across the trail, between the trees. Immediately, you sense that there's someone very important on the other side of this gate.

"As you approach the gate, it begins to open outward, and inside, you see a small table with two chairs. One chair is empty, and in the other is [*Name the person being grieved].

"As you approach the table, they greet you as their face lights up. They've got some things to tell you –some unfinished business – and I know you have some, too.

"Sit at the table with [Name]. Tell them how happy you are to see them one final time."

[Pause for a moment.]

"There are some things you want to say. What are those things you wanted to say but never got the chance? Tell them now, and give me a nod when you're done. This is your opportunity to clear your mind and let them know. Feel free to say as much as you like."

[Pause until they nod.]

"And now, they have some final things to tell you. Let them talk, and give me a nod when they're done.'

[Pause until they nod.]

"Now, as you stand up to give them one final hug goodbye, you notice for the first time that they're bound to the chair by chains. They cannot get up out of the chair.

"For you see, your eternal love for this person coupled with the intense sense of loss, has kept them bound to this world.

"In order for them to really grow and progress to whatever is next, they need to be set free – and you do, too.

"Reaching into your satchel, you find an ornate scepter, with a hilt made of carved metal, and a large glowing jewel at the end.

"This scepter is not of this world. It is powered by your love and has the ability to break bond that is holding this person back.

"Touch the scepter to the bonds and watch as they fall to the ground.

"Immediately, [Name] is free and begins floating to their feet.

"With one final embrace, they tell you they love you. Tell [Name] you love them.

"As [Name] begins walking up the trail into the mist, you know it's time for you to go as well. In releasing [Name], you've also released yourself to live your life to the fullest, in a way that honors [Name] and would make them happy.

"You make your way down the trail as the gates close behind you, thinking about how bright your future looks now."

Insomnia

"Visualize that you are a sponge being wrung of stress, down and out your toes. Take three deep breaths and "sleep now". Hear my voice only until your relaxation therapy is complete, then you will go into a deep easy natural sleep.

"Because you want to get a full night sleep, and because you want to awaken in the morning feeling completely refreshed, rested and full of pep and energy, each night as you retire you relax every muscle in your body by taking 3 deep breaths. After each breath you say to yourself *sleep now*. And let every muscle and nerve go loose and limp. After the third breath you are so completely relaxed you immediately drift off into a deep and restful slumber which remains unbroken until morning.

"Only an emergency awakens you and if this happens you return to bed after attending it and go to sleep within 60 seconds. It is easy for you to relax and go to sleep because you expect to sleep. Throughout your sleep, you are contented and pleasantly relaxed.

"You always relax completely upon taking 3 deep breaths and at bedtime you always go to sleep as you relax. You sleep soundly and comfortably and without effort. Throughout your sleep you feel calm, contented and relaxed and you carry this calm, contented sense of relaxation over into you waking hours. You always awaken at your usual rising time and feel wonderful! Completely relaxed, rested, alert and cheerful! Your eyes open, you sit up and put your feet on the floor immediately, you stretch, and you feel good. Really ready for another wonderful day. You thoroughly enjoy your deep restful sleep and at bedtime you just take 3 deep breaths and think *"sleep now"* after each breath, and you go to sleep automatically. All of these thoughts come to you when you relax and say *"sleep now"*.

"I am now going to bring you through the colors of the rainbow. The colors are red/orange, yellow/green, blue, purple/lavender, and white. As I go through the colors you will go deeper and deeper into natural sleep. On the color white you will easily and gently reach over and turn off the machine that is playing this tape. After you turn off the machine, you will go into a very deep and very relaxed state of natural, normal sleep.

"Red/orange ... slowly, calmly, easily and gently going into deep, normal sleep.

"Yellow/green ... every nerve and muscle in your body is loose and limp and relaxed, as you go deeper and deeper into natural sleep.

"Blue ... from head to toe you feel good, you feel perfect in every way, you go deeper and deeper into natural sleep.

"Purple/lavender ... your mind and your body are now going into a very deep and healthful slumber. You feel good, and at the next color, you gently and easily, without disturbing your restful slumber, reach over and turn off your machine, then you go into deep restful and natural sleep for the entire night.

"White ... easily and gently now reach over and turn off your machine that is playing this tape. *Sleep now. Sleep now. Sleep now.*"

Alcohol

"You are relaxed now, and because you are so relaxed you begin to feel free from all tensions, anxiety and fear. You now realize that you are more confident and sure of yourself because you have taken the enormous first step toward helping yourself.

"You begin to feel this strength from within, motivating you to overcome any and every obstacle that may stand in the way of your happiness, social life and home life.

"You will find that from this moment on you are developing more self-control. You will now face every situation in a calm, relaxed state of mind. Your thinking is very clear and sharp at all times.

"You begin to feel that your self-respect and confidence are expanding more and more each and every day in every way. You now realize that in the past drinking was an escape and weakness that you are replacing with confidence, strength and self-control. You are becoming a happy person now, with a positive attitude toward life. You are succeeding now, and you have all the abilities for success."

Constipation

"Go deeper and deeper to sleep. Deeper and deeper to sleep. You know that your whole gastro-intestinal system is simply a muscular tube which is coiled round and round inside your body. Various parts of this tube have various purposes, just like the specialized departments in a factory.

"The mouth is the receiving department where goods are accepted and unpacked. The throat and esophagus are the conveyer system. The stomach is a processing room in which the materials are prepared for use, and so on throughout the whole system. And finally we have the useful products which go into the body itself, and the waste products which we must eliminate.

"This whole factory has a continuous conveyer system. The tubes which make up this conveyer system are composed of rings of muscles. These muscles in their contractions and relaxation push the material along through the factory just like the assembly line chain in an automobile factory.

"When we start the relaxation at the throat, that is automatically followed by the natural rhythmic alternate relaxation and contraction of the muscle. These contractions occur in waves always traveling from the receiving room down toward the waste disposal departments.

"The wave of relaxation which we started a few minutes ago in the mouth and throat, is now moving down through the stomach towards the duodenum. Following the wave of relaxation comes the peristaltic waves - alternate relaxation and contraction of the muscles down through the stomach, the duodenum and into the intestine. Your whole intestinal tract is becoming relaxed and soon these waves will reach through the colon to the rectum.

"The colon is a kind of storage bin, just like a waste basket. We don't run to empty a waste basket every time we get something in it. We do empty it when it gets full. That is the way your body functions too. These peristaltic waves carry the waste material through the colon and into the rectum where it is stored. As soon as it becomes full, an automatic signal is sent out, and you realize you are about to have a bowel movement. As soon as you have that feeling, you go to the toilet.

"When you sit down on the toilet, the contact of your body with the toilet seat automatically sends a signal to the round muscle which keeps the valve closed the rest of the time. This round muscle we call the sphincter. The waste valve we call the anus.

"When you sit down on the toilet, the sphincter muscle relaxes. It becomes soft and flexible and stretches easily. And these waves of muscular contraction in the colon and rectum force the material out. These waves are working on down through your intestines now. And soon after you leave here you will feel the urge to have a bowel movement. When you feel this urge, go to the toilet, sit down and wait. Make no effort. Your body will take care of that part automatically and without effort. Make absolutely no effort.

"Your body can dispose of its waste material perfectly, if you do not interfere. Make no effort at all. Simply sit on the toilet and wait. The act of sitting on the toilet will be a signal to your subconscious mind. The sphincter muscle will relax. The rectum will empty itself easily and automatically.

"Every time you eat, your jaws automatically tense and relax. Eating is an automatic signal which starts the entire process in motion. You eat. Your throat swallows the food, alternately relaxing and contracting. The wavelike action proceeds all through your stomach, duodenum and intestines. Soon after eating, you feel the urge to go to the toilet. When you feel the urge, you go. The act of sitting on the toilet is automatically a signal to the sphincter muscle. It relaxes. The whole muscle relaxes. There is no effort on your part. The whole process is automatic.

"When you eat, the relaxation starts. Soon after eating, you experience the urge to go to the toilet. You go to the toilet. You go to the toilet immediately when you feel the urge. When you sit on the toilet, that is automatically a signal for the anus to relax and become soft and flexible. Then the colon automatically empties itself. There is nothing for you to do consciously but go to the toilet when you feel the urge. All the rest happens automatically and naturally.

"Shortly after you awaken, you are going to have the urge to go to the toilet. When you have that urge, go. And you will have an easy, natural bowel movement. Every time you eat, it is automatically the start of the process that will bring about an easy, natural bowel movement. When you have the urge to go to the toilet, go immediately. Your body will take care of the rest. You are going to have a bowel movement shortly after you awaken, and you will have another one after your next meal."

Pain Control

[Unless working with yourself, pain is a medical issue, and unless you are a licensed medical doctor, it is illegal working with pain control unless you have a referral from a licensed doctor. Even in the case that you can get a referral, make sure you are a certified practitioner first.]

"Pain is a warning device from your body. You do not need to be warned about your [specific pain problem] any more. You know the problem is there and you are correcting it.

"If you need to know about a change, if you need to be warned, you will feel a tingling in the area instead. You will then see that any new problem is taken care of.

"You no longer feel any pain connected with [specific pain problem] but this in no way alters your warning pain signals for any other reason.

"I want you now to concentrate a healing light in the area where you desire the pain to go away and stay away. Set up rapid and instantaneous healing with the healing light.

Feel all tension leaving the area. All pain is completely gone from the area. Feeling soothed, relaxed and painless. As though the entire area has been anesthetized without taking away any motor response what-so-ever. You have complete muscle and motor response but the area has no pain.

"Do no call back the pain. You do not need it. You do not want it. It no longer belongs to you. "

Problem Solving: The Oil Spill

"Have you ever seen what happens when they have an oil spill out at sea? What do they do? They send out a recovery team to address it. They put those barriers around all of the oil, totally surrounding it, and containing the spill. As you imagine this now, notice how the water outside the barriers continues to remain clean and clear. Also, notice that oil is lighter than water, so it rests on top of the water. And all the water underneath the oil stays clean and clear, too.

"That's a good thing because that means that the only remaining task is to remove the oil from the top of the water. By gently skimming the oil off the water, so that you can see it now disappearing as slowly or as quickly as you do, notice the feeling as the process leaves more and more of the beautiful sea to see.

"Looking at things in that light, how does it feel to think about that old problem you used to have?"

Releasing Negative Emotions: The Wicker Basket

"As you go even deeper now, I want you to imagine yourself on a wonderfully natural, perfectly green pathway. It's incredibly peaceful and tranquil. All the shades of green are vibrant and alive.

"As you look around feeling the breeze on your skin you notice that all of your favorite flowers are growing next and pathway. The breeze begins carrying the sweet smell of these flowers to your nose as the sun warms your skin. You feel incredible sense of calm coming over you.

"As you begin to walk down this pathway now, feeling as peaceful and tranquil as can be, you notice all the beauty and wonder of this amazing place. And you become aware of several smooth stones lying all around the pathway. There are so many of the stones, each one a different color, size and shape.

"You come across a large, flat boulder that looks almost like a table, and on top of that you notice a wicker basket, sitting there, as if someone had left it just for you.

"You decide to carry this basket with you, and as you put your arm through the handle you begin to lock down the pathway, enjoying your oneness with nature and the peace that comes from knowing that this is all here for you.

"Traveling further down the path you notice that there are more and more of these stones along the side of the trail. Each one is unique, and you feel attracted to these stones for some reason that you cannot explain.

"As you begin to pick up certain stones, you gently placed each and every one inside your basket. You feel the smoothness of each stone that you placed your basket. You can feel the warmth of each one, having been baking in the sun all afternoon.

"Continuing to walk down the pathway, you hear the faint clicking as each and every stone gently taps of the others resting there in the basket. Looking down the basket you notice the collection of rocks is getting larger.

"As you continue to walk deeper and deeper into this garden you gather more and more of the small, smooth stones, each one unique, each one attracting you in a new and different way.

"Continuing down the pathway you come to a clearing with a small, clear, beautiful, blue pond. Around the edge of the water is a fine, almost powder-like white sand, warmed by the beautiful sun, and leading into the most perfectly clear, clean, cleansing the water that you've ever seen.

"Walk over to the water's edge. As you sit down in the warm sand, you can feel your feet sinking ever so slightly and you notice your reflection in the water. Studying your own image, looking so very closely at it now, see yourself just as you are and notice every detail about yourself. You notice that you are not as happy and carefree as you'd always hoped you would be.

"A soft, warm breeze begins to blow gently through the air and it causes the pond to begin to ripple until your concentration is broken away from your reflection. As each and every ripple washes up on the sand, you feel yourself becoming more and more relaxed, and you find your attention drawn toward the wicker basket, full of smooth stones.

"Reaching down and picking up the basket, you notice how heavy it is. So heavy. And you begin to wonder why you hadn't noticed how heavy it was while you're carrying it, up until this point.

"It's so heavy in fact, that you must set it down on the bank of the pond next you to take out the stones within.

"Pick up the first stone. Feel it in your hands and examine it carefully, now. Feel it, look at, and as you turn it over notice that there's something written on the bottom of the small stone, in capital letters. It's the word ANGER. As you begin to get curious about each and every stone now, you realize there's something written on all of them.

"You decide to read each one, and to rid yourself of the undesirable ones so they no longer weigh you down.

"First, take the one that says ANGER and toss it into the middle of the pond. Hear it plop as it hits the surface of the water as that stone quickly sinks to the bottom. When the rippling stops you know the anger is at the bottom of the pond and you begin to feel lighter.

"The next is SADNESS. And because you have no desire to feel sad you cast the stone into the middle of the pond, knowing that it too is sinking to the very bottom of the pond. And as it sinks, the pond ripples. And as the last ripple hits the sand, you free yourself by letting go of all of the sadness you ever felt over the years. And you begin to feel lighter. And in feeling lighter you know and realize there's absolutely nothing to feel sad about.

"Next, take the one that says FEAR and toss it into the middle of the pond. Hear it splash into the water as that stone quickly sinks all the way down. When the water calms you know the fear is at the bottom of the pond and you feel even lighter.

"The next one is labeled HURT. Then GUILT. And the next, FRUSTRATION. Followed by JEALOUSY, JUDGEMENT, EGO, ENVY, RESENTMENT... and with each and every stone, and each and every emotion, you toss them into the center of the pond, and in doing so cast out of your life all of the negative emotion at all undesirable characteristics actions and attitudes, allowing them to disappear to the depths of his cleansing. And in doing so, you feel lighter. And in feeling lighter you know what realize there's absolutely nothing to feel bad about.

"As you are cleansed, you feel lighter and lighter as a huge weight has been lifted off your shoulders. Allow that light feeling to flow through your body now, and as it flows through your body is emotionally, spiritually and mentally relieved.

"As water stops rippling, you look into the depths of the water. Stand up and look at the very center of the pond, as you do, notice that there is no trace of the stones.

"Realizing the incredible power of this pond, you toss the entire basket into its center. Watch as the basket disappears in a huge splash, and the ripples make their way to the shore.

"And as the last ripples begin to cross the sand now, you feel lighter. And in feeling lighter you know and realize that in this life – this <u>one</u> life – that you will live each and every day with purpose, choosing only to feel alive and wonderful. Each and every day you are alive, now becomes, "the best day ever!" As you strive to make each day better than the last.

"Now as the water returns to its glassy stillness, you gaze into the reflection, and again you see the reflection of yourself. Only this time, void of the heaviness and emotion that held you back for so long. Notice that you look so confident, so self-assured, and so ready to get on with the joys of your life."

Self Confidence I

"You are relaxed now, and because you are so relaxed you begin to feel free from all tension, anxiety, and fear. You now realize that you are more confident and sure of yourself because you have taken the enormous first step to helping yourself.

"You begin to feel this strength from within, motivating you to overcome any and every obstacle that may stand in the way of your happiness, social life and home life. You will find that from this moment on you are developing more self-control. You will now face every situation in a calm and relaxed state of mind. Your thinking is very clear and sharp at all times

"You begin to feel that your self-respect and confidence are expanding more and more each day in every way. You now realize that in the past you felt helpless and overwhelmed and you are replacing that with confidence, strength and self-control. You are becoming a happy person now with a positive attitude towards life. You are succeeding now in all that you do and you have all the abilities necessary for success."

[Explain value judging and resisting.]

"Realize that unhappy relationships are caused by value judging and resisting yourself and others. Love is a natural state of being and you are naturally in a state of loving when you accept yourself and others totally and unconditionally. Realize that you do not have to approve of anyone's actions, behavior or appearance in order to willingly accept and love them. Our actions are but the means we choose to satisfy our dominant needs to feel good. You feel warm and loving towards yourself and others, despite any undesired actions, behavior or appearance."

Stop Smoking Script

"And just drifting down, deeper and deeper, now… It can be relaxing and even educational to watch a masterpiece being built – a thing of beauty; A thing of strength; A thing of the most articulate nature. And I wonder if you know what's involved in building a cocoon – a place of protection, change and metamorphosis. I don't know everything involved, but I remember watching as a child, as a very unremarkable caterpillar came to the realization that… it's time for a change.

"It's time to take the steps necessary to cast away the unremarkable exterior and allow the beauty that lives inside to come out. The cater pillar surveyed his surroundings, looking for the right way to go about this – obvious that safety and health are the primary concerns.

"And so I watched… as the caterpillar began weaving its silk – uncommonly strong and amazingly resilient, yet flexible – around the stem of a sturdy leaf. Winding around, and round and round… doing what it must to build a solid foundation for change.

"Around, and around, and around…

"And now, as you imagine yourself walking through that valley of relaxation, you come across the majestic, sheer face of a small mountain made entirely from marble. Noticing a round entrance situated in the center of this mountain, you move your feet across the graven walkway and begin to wander inside.

"As you make your way down the round hallway, ribbed with arches every few yards, you can hear the wind at your back and feel it moving past you… in and out, like the waves of the ocean. Moving on, you come to a fork in the hallway leading to two dirty, musty, dimly lit chambers. You immediately realize that these chambers were once amazingly beautiful.

"Seeing a mop, a sponge and a bucket against the far wall, you begin to go to work on a small area of the chamber. The beautifully intricate patterns of pink marble with red veins immediately begins to unfold before your eyes – it's absolutely beautiful, just as you expected. And while you'd love to stop and study it, you've got a lot more work to do. So you scrub, rinse and dry one area, then move to the next as more and more of the beautifully pristine chambers become visible. Scrub, rinse, dry… scrub, rinse, dry. And as your conscious mind continues – scrub, rinse, dry… scrub, rinse, dry…

"Imagine yourself, now, standing in a warm, shallow pond of sparkling, pure, absolutely clean water. This is the most pure, cleansing water you've ever seen. In front of you is a tall waterfall, and the water comes down in a smooth, undisturbed sheet, glistening and barely rippling the still water of the pond. And as you move closer, you begin to see a mirror image in the glassy waterfall… It's a reflection of the perfectly healthy, smoke-free you – a reflection of perfection.

"This reflection is healthy and happy, inside and out, and as you approach the waterfall, you stretch your palms outward until they meet those of your reflection of perfection. Feeling the warm water as your fingertips intersect with your reflection, just imagine all the nicotine, tar and other carcinogens in your fingertips being washed away. As you continue to move forward, merging and becoming one with your reflection of perfection, notice as all the nicotine, tar and other carcinogens wash away from your lower arms, all the way up to your elbows, leaving behind only an energetic, vibrant, naturally healthy, you.

"You can feel the goosebumps rising all over your body as the sound of the waterfall becomes louder and you greet the smiling face of your reflection."

[DIRECT COMMANDS]

"In a few moments, I'm going to offer you some suggestions. You will find these suggestions easy to enjoy, and easy to accept. You will accept them because, when you act on these suggestions, you will achieve greater levels of health and well-being. By accepting these suggestions, you will preserve your body more effectively and your job to stay healthy will be much, much easier.

"From this point forward, you are a non-smoker. You easily and effortlessly turn down cigarettes – not only because you're a non-smoker, but also because you simply don't want cigarettes. If someone is smoking around you, the smoke may or may not bother you, but in any case, it won't make you want a cigarette, because smoke doesn't do that to non-smokers, and you're a non-smoker. Again, you're a non-smoker now... You cherish your lungs, mouth and skin, and you'll never again subject them to the torture of a cigarette.

"For a week or so after your last cigarette, if you crave sugar or feel dehydrated, realize that this is a natural reaction and does not mean you need a cigarette. These are not nicotine withdrawals, but natural reactions while your body adjusts your blood sugar levels and rehydrates your cells. So, rather than eating junk food and drinking colas or coffee eat fresh fruit and drink a healthy supply of water. The fruit will help ease low blood-sugar and the water will help to rehydrate your cells. Again, if you find yourself craving sweet or fluids, you will satisfy those cravings with fresh fruits and water.

"Secondly, one of the benefits of smoking is that it forces smokers to take short breaks from work, family, stress, etc, and perhaps even to spend some time outside. To avoid that benefit from attracting you back to smoking, and to alleviate situations where nervous energy may build up, you'll take as many breaks and spend as much time outside as you did before our session. You'll continue to give yourself breaks and time outside, but as a non-smoker."

[END DIRECT COMMANDS]

"Taking one more step, now, the warm water begins washing the nicotine and other toxins away from your upper arms, and the front of your legs and torso. Already you feel healthier. Your posture and demeanor are now that of a naturally trim, active, healthy person.

"One more step… the water washes comfortably over your face, head, shoulders, torso, hips and down to your legs, taking with it all the toxins your body doesn't need. And as you take that final step through, the water cleanses your entire body, and you find yourself standing in the second chamber, dry and relaxed, feeling healthier and more energetic than you have felt in a very long time.

"And you continue now to clean up the last few inches of the chamber… Scrub, rinse, dry… scrub, rinse, dry… Scrub, rinse, dry…

"You look over the chamber and smile to yourself with satisfaction as you realize that you've completed your task and cleaned every inch of these chambers, and they are beautiful. Yet, your job is not done. You will continue to work at keeping these chambers clean and beautiful, making sure that they never again get so filthy and musty.

And as you continue to watch the cocoon, you begin to notice some movement, as the most amazing butterfly begins emerging. And as you realize how easily and naturally change occurs, the butterfly, completely transformed and metamorphosized, begins taking flight."

Taking Action and Making a Difference: The Starfish

"An old man took a walk along the beach one morning. The full moon lit the beach as the faint orange glow of the sun was just beginning to show along the horizon. Dawn was approaching.

"As he continued his leisurely walk along the beach, hearing the waves washing in and out along the shore, he saw a man dancing on the beach.

"As he walked closer, he rubbed his weary eyes and saw that the man wasn't a dancer at all. He was running along the beach picking up starfish and flinging them into the sea.

"The old man approached the younger man and asked, "Why are you spending so much energy doing what seems to be such a waste of time?"

171

"The younger man explained that these starfish were stuck. They confused motion with progress and thought they were getting somewhere. But they became stranded on the beach and the sun was fast approaching. If he didn't do something about it, they would surely die.

"The old man said, "But there must be thousands of miles of beaches and millions of starfish. How could your effort make any difference?"

"The young man looked down at the starfish in his hand and smiled, and as he tossed it safely back into the ocean, he exclaimed, "It makes a difference to this one!"

Weight Reduction Script

"And, just drifting down... deeper and deeper, now... It can be relaxing and even educational to watch a masterpiece being built - A thing of beauty; A thing of strength; A thing of the most articulate nature. And I wonder if you know what's involved in building a cocoon - A place of protection, change and metamorphosis.

"I don't know everything involved, but I remember watching as a child, as a very unremarkable caterpillar came to the realization that... *it's time for a change.* It's time to *take the steps necessary* to *cast away the unremarkable exterior* and *allow the beauty that lives inside to come out.* The caterpillar surveyed his surroundings, looking for the right way to go about this - obvious that *safety and health are the primary concern.*

"And so I watched... as the caterpillar began weaving its silk - uncommonly strong and amazingly resilient, yet flexible - around the stem of a sturdy leaf. Winding round, and round, and round... doing what it must to *build a solid foundation for change.*

"Around, and around, and around...

"And as the caterpillar works, I'm going to speak directly now to *your unconscious* mind, while your conscious mind idly contemplates the patterns of glistening silk going round, and round and round..."

[DIRECT COMMANDS]

"For the first seven days of this weight reduction program, you will carry the included notepad with you, everywhere you go. Diligently write down every piece of food and every bit of liquid you consume - no matter how small or insignificant it may seem. Crumbs of food and drops of fluid count. Candy, too. Write down the date, the time, the location, what you ate and drank, and how much. Realize how different the list is from your perception of how much you **thought** you consumed before starting this program.

"Again, for the first seven days of this program, you will make notes about everything you eat and drink, noting the date and time, the location, what you ate and drank, and how much of each. You will do this for seven days from the date you start this program. "Doing so will become habit, quickly and effortlessly. Reflect often on ways you can improve your general diet.

"And now, as you imagine yourself standing in front of a large, steel door - heavy... cold... and thick... , you notice with a few beeps and clicks that a motor whirs and the door begins opening away from you... revealing a room filled from ceiling to floor, as far as you can see, with vastly powerful, humming computer systems. As you make your way down the five steps of the short stairway at the entrance, a sign catches your eye. It says, "*You are in Control* Room Number One."

"As you approach the console and look at the dials and knobs, you realize that at one point, you knew <u>exactly</u> how to use all this equipment, but you've been away for a very long time, and the settings have gotten out of balance. Looking around, you see a big, heavy-bound dusty book with the words "Instructions" embossed on the cover. This is *your* instruction manual.

"Inside, you see the ideal setting for a control, switch or knob on each page. There's one for happiness - go ahead and crank it <u>way</u> up - one for procrastination - turn that one down - a page for metabolism, one for heart rate, one for body temperature, and so on.

"Each time you flip to the next page, you adjust the settings to reflect the perfect, healthy you. And as your conscious mind flips through those pages and makes adjustments, I'm going to speak directly to *your unconscious* mind. Your conscious mind can just continue to flip-read adjust, flip-read-adjust, flip-read-adjust. It can choose to listen in, if it wants, or it can just drift... and... Flip-read-adjust, flip-read-adjust, flip-read-adjust."

[DIRECT SUGGESTIONS]

"In a few seconds, I'm going to offer you two suggestions. You will find these suggestions easy to enjoy, and easy to accept. You will accept them because when you act on these suggestions, you will achieve greater levels of health. By accepting these suggestions, you will preserve your body more effectively, and your job to stay healthy will be much, much easier.

"First, realizing that good health starts with good digestion, and good digestion begins in the mouth, begin chewing your food slower and longer than ever before. Chew every bite you take six to ten percent longer. Chew your food slower and longer than ever before. By doing so, your food will be more properly digested when it enters the stomach. This allows the stomach to continue to digest the food so that it gets into your intestines properly, and the vitamins and nutrients from the food can be absorbed easily, giving you higher levels energy - the kind of energy you need to help you do what you know you need to do in order to become healthier and to achieve your goals easily and effortlessly.

And chewing your food longer and slower will allow you to pull more flavor from your food and help you to enjoy it more. This enjoyment will fulfill you more than the food itself, so you will eat less food but still get the same amount of pleasure - maybe even more than ever before.

"Secondly, realizing that you don't need to be absolutely full to fulfill your dietary needs, you will check your stomach after you have swallowed each bite, and before you prepare to take the next. On a scale of one to ten, with one being absolutely starving and ten being absolutely full, you'll check your stomach after each bite and stop at the number six or seven. This will leave you pleasantly satisfied, but not uncomfortably full.

"Again, you will immediately begin chewing your food six to ten percent slower than you normally do, taking time to enjoy each bite. You'll check your stomach after each bite, and you'll stop eating at six or seven on a scale of one to ten, with one being absolutely starving and ten being absolutely full.

"Imagine yourself, now, standing in a warm, shallow pond of sparkling, pure, absolutely clean water. In front of you is a tall waterfall, and the water comes down in a smooth, undisturbed sheet, glistening and barely rippling the still water of the pond. And as you move closer, you begin to see a mirror image in the glassy waterfall... It is a reflection of the perfect you - a reflection of perfection. I'm not necessarily talking about the kind of body that society tells us is perfect... I'm talking about your own interpretation of where you want to be with regards to health… because whatever that is… it's just perfect… that's the reflection of perfection you see in the waterfall. Make it as attractive inside as it is on the outside.

"Approaching the waterfall, you stretch your palms outward until they meet those of your reflection of perfection. Feeling the warm water as your fingertips intersect with your refection, just imagine all the excess fat in your fingertips being washed away. As you continue to move forward, merging and becoming one with your reflection of perfection, notice as all the excess fat washes away from your lower arms, all the way up to your elbows, leaving behind only a healthy, vibrant, naturally trim you. You can feel the goosebumps rising all over your body as the sound of the waterfall becomes louder and you greet the smiling face of your reflection.

"Taking one more step, the warm water begins washing the excess fat away from your upper arms and the front of your legs and torso. Already, you feel lighter and more healthy. Your posture is now that of a naturally trim, attractive person. One more step... the water washes comfortably over your face, head shoulders, torso, hips and down your legs, taking with it all the excess fat your body doesn't need. And as you take that final step through, the water cleanses your entire body, and you find yourself standing in the control room, dry and relaxed, feeling healthier and lighter than you have felt in a very long time.

"And as you continue now with the last few pages... Flip-read-adjust, flip-read-adjust, flip-read-adjust...

"You look over the vast control boards and smile to yourself with satisfaction as you realize that you've completed your task and adjusted each and every control to create a healthier you. Yet your job is not done. You will continually monitor and adjust these settings, making sure that they never again get so far out of balance.

"And one final suggestion, which you'll happily and easily accept... Each time you hear my voice, on an audio program or in person, you will readily and happily accept my suggestions, and when we do hypnosis in the future you'll re-enter this wonderfully comfortable and relaxed state, but deeper and deeper than ever before.

"And as you head toward the door to exit the control room, you will climb five stairs. With each stair you climb, you'll become more aware, more alert, returning to a wakeful state, and feeling wonderful and refreshed."

**More scripts are available on the internet.

Appendix IV: Bibliography - Other Books and Products

Books

Hypnosis

- Hypnotherapy and Hypnosis by Calvin S. Banyan, Gerald F. Kein, Calvin D. Banyan

- The New Encyclopedia of Stage Hypnosis by Ormond McGill

- The Wizard Within: The Krazner Method of Hypnotherapy by A. M. Krazner

- Tranceworks by Michael D. Yapko

- Handbook of Hypnotic Suggestions and Metaphors by Corydon Hammond, et al

- Fun with Hypnosis: The Complete How-To Guide by Professor Svengali

- Training Trances by John Overdurf, Julie Silverthorn

- Trance-Formations by Richard Bandler and John Grinder

Self-Hypnosis

- The Complete Idiot's Guide to Hypnosis by Roberta Temes

- Hypnosis for Change by Josie Hadley, Carol Staudacher

Neuro Linguistic Programming (NLP)

- The Magic of NLP Demystified: A Pragmatic Guide to Communication and Change by Byron A. Lewis, et al

- Neuro-Linguistic Programming: Volume I by Robert Dilts, John Grinder, Richard Bandler, and Judith DeLozier

- Patterns of the Hypnotic Techniques of Milton H. Erickson Volume I by Richard Bandler and John Grinder

- Patterns of the Hypnotic Techniques of Milton H. Erickson Volume II by Richard Bandler and John Grinder

- The Structure of Magic Volume I by Richard Bandler and John Grinder

- The Structure of Magic Volume II by Richard Bandler and John Grinder

- The Sourcebook of Magic by L. Michael Hall

- Modeling with NLP by Robert Dilts

- Changing Belief Systems by Robert Dilts

- Using your Brain… For a Change by Richard Bandler, et al

- Heart of the Mind by Richard Bandler, et al

- Reframing by Richard Bandler and John Grinder

- Therapeutic Metaphors by David A. Gordon

- Frogs into Princes by Richard Bandler and John Grinder

- Personality Selling: Using NLP and the Enneagram to Understand People and How They Are Influenced by Albert J. Valentino

- Instant Rapport by Michael Brooks

Motivational

- My Voice will Go With You: The Motivational Tales of Milton H. Erickson

- Chicken Soup for the Soul and other related titles by Jack Canfield

Music for Hypnosis

- Hypnotic TranceScapes Volume I – Mystical Forest
  Specially designed by the Author of Learn
  Hypnosis… Now! and royalty free once purchased
  for you to use in recordings of your own.

- Across an Ocean of Dreams by 2002

- Wrapped in Stillness by Various Artists

Appendix V: Agreement for Use of Hypnosis MP3

By listening to the hypnosis audio included as a bonus in this book, you agree that this MP3 is provided as-is and without warrantee for educational purposes only. You also agree to the following instructions:

1. Do not listen while driving
2. Do not listen while doing anything that requires your attention
3. Find a comfortable place to <u>sit</u> (not lying down)
4. Sit in a place of relative silence where you won't be disturbed
5. This is for personal use only. You agree not to sell, give away or publicly broadcast the file.

You also agree to hold harmless and indemnify both Transform Destiny and Michael Stevenson against any and all claims and actions arising out of the listening to this audio, including, without limitation, expenses, judgments, fines, settlements and other amounts actually and reasonably incurred in connection with any liability, suit, action, loss, or damage arising or resulting from your participation in listening to this audio.

If you have any psychological or psychiatric diagnoses, you agree to not use this MP3 until consulting with your licensed professional (if you do not agree you may not listen to the file, so please delete the file without listening now).